FROM

LANDA

1 - 2 - 98

BENEDETTO PISTRUCCI PRINCIPAL ENGRAVER AND CHIEF MEDALLIST OF THE ROYAL MINT.

1783-1855.

MICHAEL. A. MARSH

MICHAEL. A. MARSH (PUBLICATIONS)
25A ST NEOTS ROAD
HARDWICK
CAMBRIDGESHIRE
CB3 7QH

First Edition 1996
Reprinted 1998

Printed by Black Bear Press Ltd,
King's Hedges Road, Cambridge, CB4 2PQ
Tel: (01223) 424571 Fax: (01223) 426877

ISBN: 0 9506929 2 1

CONTENTS

Page No

Introduction.   1

Chapter 1.   2
Biographical Sources. Family origins. Benedetto's education.
Rome. Mango, Tofanelli and the fight.

Chapter 2.   7
Desalief, Cerbara, Morelli. Important alteration. Marriage and a family.
The Grand Duchess Baciocchi. Florence, Rome and the eye problem.

Chapter 3.   12
Bonelli. Paris and on to England. Problems. König. Illness. Flora
incident. No 8 Panton Square. Introduction to Sir Joseph Banks.

Chapter 4.   16
The Mint. William Wellesley Pole. The New Coinage. The Sovereign.
The Reducing Machine. Mint residence for Benedetto, and more illness.

Chapter 5.   23
Two important commissions, the Elgin Marbles and the Waterloo Medal.
George IV Coronation. The New Coinage. Pole resigns. Chantrey
incident and Merlen.

Chapter 6.   29
Carl Friedrich Voigt. George Tierney M.P. new Master. Pistrucci
Chief Medallist. Camillo and Raphael. Cameos and Medals.

Chapter 7.   35
The Fothergillian Medal. William IV. Sculpture. Medals and Cameos.

Chapter 8.   43
Thomas Marquis Pistrucci. Victoria Coronation. The Duchy of
Lancaster Seal. Pistrucci's "Invention". Benvenuto final child.
Chief Engraver, Rome. Return to England.

Chapter 9.   47
Medals. Gladstone, new Master. Completion of the Waterloo Medal
Matrices. "Fine Arts Cottage", Numismatic Chronicle correspondence 1849.

Chapter 10.   58
Move to "Flora Lodge". The Pistruccis in Australia. Pistrucci's final
work. Conclusion.

Plates Index

All items are the work of Benedetto Pistrucci except where otherwise stated.

Plate No		Page No
1.	Wax model of Napoleon I.	64
2.	Payne-Knights Flora cameo.	65
3.	George III jasper cameo for the Sovereign.	66
4.	George III jasper cameo for the Shilling.	67
5.	George III jasper cameo for the Half-crown.	68
6.	George III gold Sovereign 1817.	69
7.	George III gold Five pounds 1820 (Proof).	70
8.	George III gold Two pounds 1820 (Proof).	71
9.	George III silver Crown 1818 ANNO REGNI LVIII.	72
10.	Original letter written by Pistrucci in 1818.	73
11.	The Waterloo Medal Matrices.	74 - 75
12.	Wax model of the Waterloo Medal.	76
13.	Wax model of the Waterloo Medal.	77
14.	George IV gold Coronation Medal 1821.	78
15.	George IV gold Sovereign 1825.	79

Plates Index

Plate No   **Page No**

16. George IV silver Crown 1821.   80

17. Uniface portrait plaque of Benedetto Pistrucci   82
     by C. F. Voigt 1826. (Royal Mint)

18. Uniface portrait plaque of Benedetto Pistrucci   83
     by C. F. Voigt 1826. (Baden Cabinet)

19. Death of Taylor Combe Medal 1826.   84

20. Death of Duke of York Medal 1827.   85

21. Royal Humane Society Medal 1839.   86

22. Sir Gilbert Blane Medal 1830.   87

23. Victoria Long Service and Good Conduct Medal.   88

24. Duke of Wellington marble bust 1832.   89

25. Self-portrait bust of Benedetto Pistrucci.   90

26. The Princess Victoria cameo.   91

27. The Princess Victoria cameo (No 26) set in gold engraved   92
     plate and in fitted leather box.

28. Napoleon cameo mounted in gold on a snuff box.   93

29. Amalthea and the infant Zeus cameo.   94

30. George, Prince Regent cameo.   95

Plates Index

Plate No		Page No
31.	Head of a Child cameo (Daughter of Billing).	96
32.	Duke of Wellington shell cameo by Raphael Pistrucci.	97
33.	George III cameo set in gold pendant.	98
34.	Victoria gold Coronation Medal 1838.	99
35.	Duke of Wellington Laudatory Medal 1841.	100
36.	Flora Lodge. Pistrucci's last home. The author.	101
37.	Flora Lodge. Pistrucci's last home. Tom Pistrucci.	102
38.	Benvenuto Pistrucci in Australia c.1900.	103
39.	Napoleon III visit to England. Wax model.	104
40.	Napoleon III visit to England. Wax model.	105
41.	The grave of Benedetto Pistrucci at Virginia Water.	106
42.	The grave of Benedetto Pistrucci at Virginia Water.	107
43.	The Burial Register of Virginia Water Church.	108
44.	A street map of Rome showing via Pistrucci.	109
45.	William Wellesley Pole Medal 1823.	110
46.	Obverse die of the Pole Medal 1823.	111
47.	Lead trial striking of the obverse of the Pole Medal 1823.	112

Plates Index

Plate No   **Page No**

48. Roman Emperor Augustus cameo.   113

49. Electrotypes of the Waterloo Medal. Obverse.   114

50. Electrotypes of the Waterloo Medal. Reverse.   115

51. The Waterloo Medal. Brown wax impression. 1980 Obverse.   116

52. The Waterloo Medal. Brown wax impression. 1980 Reverse.   117

53. St. George slaying the Dragon. Wax model for the Sovereign.   118

54. The Benedetto Pistrucci Medal   119
     by Avril Vaughan and John Lobban 1993-94.

55. A proud moment for Tom Pistrucci   120
     at the Royal Mint, London 1986.

56. The author, The Deputy Chief Engraver of the Royal Mint   121
     Derek Gorringe, Tom Pistrucci and the Reducing Machine
     at the Mint 1986.

57. Tom Pistrucci admiring the Waterloo Medal Matrices.   122

ACKNOWLEDGMENTS

I would like to begin by offering my sincere thanks to those who have kindly assisted me in the compilation of this book. Without doubt their help has, I am sure, created a better book. To the following I say thank you very much, your efforts and time were much appreciated,

The Royal Mint
The British Museum, London
The Fitzwilliam Museum, Cambridge
The Victoria and Albert Museum, London
The Ashmolean Museum, Oxford
National Museums and Galleries Merseyside. Liverpool Museum
Hancocks & Co (Jewellers) Ltd, London
Mr. M. F. Howard
Mr. J. G. Pollard
Mr. S. Warren
Mr. G. P. Dyer, Librarian and Curator, The Royal Mint
Mr. F. Bird (Photographer)
Mrs. M. Story
Mr. Christopher Eimer
Herr Klaus Sommer

MICHAEL A. MARSH

Introduction

My fascination for the gold sovereign began many years ago, and probably reached culmination in 1980 when I published my book *The Gold Sovereign*. The coin itself has always had a sort of magnetic attraction to me, and it seemed inevitable that the name of Benedetto Pistrucci would soon come very much to the fore. Had it not been for the Italian engraver we may never have had the modern sovereign, certainly not his wonderful creation of St. George slaying the Dragon.

Over the last thirty years I have accumulated quite a dossier of information relating to Pistrucci, and I feel the time has come when I can turn this collection of many separate papers, notes and various references into a worthwhile history of one of our most outstanding engravers. I do not believe a comprehensive history of Pistrucci has been written before, and in any event not in the English language. This I feel is a shame because I sense that there are many who would like to read about this quite remarkable Italian who spent so much of his life at the Royal Mint, and who finally died in England.

Chapter 1

Back in 1875 Archibald Billing's book, *The Science of Gems, Jewels, Coins and Medals* gave us useful information on Benedetto Pistrucci, and it also contains a part autobiography by Pistrucci in which he tells in the main about his early years. Billing and Pistrucci were great friends. Then in 1906 there was an entry in the *Biographical Dictionary of Medallists* by L. Forrer which contained many useful facts and details relating to Pistrucci. In more recent years there have been two further publications of real interest on Pistrucci, the first of which in 1981 was an excellent short history entitled *Benedetto Pistrucci in Inghilterra* and this was written by J. Graham Pollard, and then in 1989 there were two magnificent volumes of the *Bollettino Di Numismatica* by Lucia Pirzio Biroli Stefanelli, and these contain many excellent plates of the Pistrucci wax models that have survived; they are in the Museo Della Zecca in Rome though both the last publications I mention were written in Italian.

Benedetto Pistrucci was born in Rome on the 24 May 1783[1]; his father Frederico and mother Antonia Greco were both Romans. Frederico held the position of Senior Judge to the High Criminal Court of Rome, and as the holder of several other important positions he was certainly able to provide well for the Pistrucci family. The family consisted of Philip the first born, Benedetto the next and finally Catherine; sadly she died at only 21 years of age.

When it was time for the young Pistruccis to begin their education Frederico had very fixed ideas that the family should follow in his own footsteps; it was not to be, and Philip even when only four years old was showing an inclination towards the art of painting. Benedetto had little or no interest in study of any kind, and none whatsoever in Latin. However, as we shall see, Philip's ambition to be a painter and the boys' obvious closeness as brothers would prove in the future to be invaluable towards the greatness the young Benedetto was to achieve. So the Latin struggle for Benedetto continued, and can best be explained by his own words from his part autobiography in Billing:- "At length by the efforts of so many teachers, I acquired a little Latin, somewhat after the manner of a parrot".

---

1   Year of birth was confirmed by Church records of Virginia Water in 1986, and birth certificate. Many times in the past this was incorrectly stated as 1784.

Perhaps with some relief from the point of view of his studies fate was to interrupt in general the life of the Pistrucci family, and this was brought about by the invasion of Italy by the French. The family were forced to leave Bologna and seek sanctuary in Rome because of the invasion of Italy by the French led by Napoleon.

With the loss of all their property in Bologna the family took root in Rome, and soon Benedetto found himself in the Roman College to resume his study of Latin! He was at this time just eleven years of age, and of course, his interest in Latin had not improved. I feel it was at this point that the very first indication of his real talent was to appear, and he began to work with his hands. Again his own words from Billing are well worth repeating:- "He (father) sent me to study Latin which was as disagreeable to me as ever; and, instead of applying myself to it, I amused myself by making little toys of wood, such as cars, cannon etc.; in short I was never without tools in my hand, some of which I had made myself". There was little doubt that Pistrucci was displaying a real interest in mechanics, and he was well praised for his "little works".

Further interruption to the Pistrucci family life was however brought about once more when Napoleon continued his advance. The family were to move again and this time in the direction of Naples. However, short of Naples the decision was made to stop in Frosinone, and on their arrival they learned that Napoleon had offered 1000 louis to whomsoever should bring him the head of Frederico Pistrucci. The decision to stay on in Frosinone was made, and it was not long before Benedetto realised that the city had Latin schools, so for him this stop-over might yet again involve him in his much hated study of Latin. The Latin schools in Frosinone were indeed excellent and both the young Pistruccis were quickly sent to one.

As ever there was no improvement in Benedetto's efforts at Latin whereas Philip excelled as usual, and as a result he was granted permission by his father to take up a position with a local painter called Mango, who was an artist quite well known for his landscapes, and so Philip was able to follow his love of painting. As a result of this move Benedetto became very despondent at having to remain on his own at the Latin school, and finally his father allowed him to join Philip at the house of Mango, although he feared that Benedetto would not do any better at drawing. But this assumption was to prove wrong and Benedetto began drawing in earnest, and attempted to draw with crayon in real detail the parts of the human eye. At first he found this was not easy but at last the will to achieve something began to appear, and he produced more examples which began to attract the interest of Mango, and praise was soon to follow. Mango also noted his strong inclination for mechanism, which of course was to prove a considerable asset in what was soon to come. Before long Mango told him of a brother of his in Rome who was an engraver of cameos, and it was at this point that the mind of Benedetto was fully made up; he knew exactly that he wanted to become an engraver of gems. He lost no time in telling his father of his feelings but he met with little positive response. In any event the French were still a problem, and so once again an obstruction to Benedetto's career had appeared. However, the Pope made peace with the French, and so the Pistruccis were able to return to Rome, and yes, the inevitable occurred, and Benedetto was sent to study Latin! After his usual failure with the subject, and his falling out with literally everyone at the college Frederico decided to end what had now become a dangerous as well as farcical situation. He allowed Benedetto to take up a position with Guiseppe Mango the cameo cutter who was the brother of the painter from Frosinone. Benedetto now nearly thirteen years old was immediately put to work drawing and was very soon praised by Mango. But after a few months he took the advice of his brother Philip and approached his master the great Stefano Tofanelli, a superb painter and designer. Tofanelli was very impressed with Benedetto's drawings and took much interest in him, giving him lessons and a great deal of advice.

In less than a year his progress was so noticeable that Mango began to expect more of him, and he was asked to do drawings of cameos that he was making, especially those with figures on them. Mango told him he was being asked to do this to improve his drawing in miniature. Although a year had gone by and he had reached the age of fourteen he felt very much that he was really only being exploited by Mango, and so he decided to spend more and more time under Tofanelli, even to the extent of working for him at night and in total very long hours. By this time Benedetto's enthusiasm for his chosen profession was so strong that even on Sundays, after their religious duties were finished, he and Philip went to the Vatican where they spent endless hours admiring and studying the great works of Raphael and Michelangelo. Indeed the masterpieces that were to follow in the years ahead show clear evidence of the study that Benedetto found so interesting and alluring at the Vatican.

After several months of really hard endeavour where his progress became even more apparent to Mango, Benedetto was given several ordinary flints to cut by Mango, and these were stones that had a hard foundation but were also of a very fine consistency. This type of stone enabled very defined and beautiful work to be put on it. Pistrucci cut many of these, and the results were so good that Mango sold them at a very good profit, and undoubtedly took the full credit for them. He certainly never gave his apprentice any money for such marvellous efforts.

At this time Benedetto was to suffer yet another major upset in his young career, but as we shall see again from adversity he made a substantial gain to add yet more to his already considerable talent. Mango had three other young men working under him at that time who were obviously jealous of Benedetto's talent, and Mango himself inflamed the situation by making no secret of the fact that Pistrucci's work cost him nothing. So why should he give work to the others? One of these youths named Giuseppino was so incensed by this that he deliberately began an argument with Benedetto, and this was quickly followed by a vicious attack on him in which a sharp tool from the workshop was plunged into his abdomen. Though badly wounded Benedetto struck back at his assailant causing him to flee. How would this young boy occupy himself as he lay ill for several weeks recovering at home? He bought some wax and taught himself to model with it, so even though ill and in pain this already brilliant brain intended not to remain idle. It is appropriate at this point to explain how in the years that were to follow this newly acquired skill assisted Benedetto so much in his method of work. First it has to be said that there were few others who could model in bees-wax as well as Pistrucci, and the models of his that survive in the Museo Della Zecca of Rome are a clear indication of his brilliant talent at modelling in wax.

Not all engravers worked from a model created from bees-wax indeed there were some who never mastered the art, and so they used other methods -

perhaps just working from a drawing. However, once the young Pistrucci had perfected his own use of it he realised what an asset it would be to his future, and in fact from that time he was never without a ball of wax in his pocket. This is a good juncture at which to explain exactly Pistrucci's procedure when starting on a commission. First and foremost if his subject was a living person he preferred to work from a real life sitting, and no matter who it was this was his method, and very seldom would he work in any other way. Many important people gave Pistrucci personal sittings, and probably none more readily than Queen Victoria, who did so on several occasions and indeed had a great affection for him. Pistrucci was seldom known to work from a drawing, and preferred to work from his own wax models. Usually he worked his wax on a piece of slate, and if the subject was a human he would first model him or her in nude form, because in doing this he felt he could get the figure exact, next he would add whatever robes or dress that was necessary along with any other embellishments. Many times Pistrucci was able to and would work from just one wax, then again it is known that there were times when he would produce three waxes for one commission. Certainly on one occasion he worked from three separate waxes of Queen Victoria. To conclude the account of Pistrucci's mode of work it is well worth while to move forward a few years to 1838. At this point a further clarification of Pistrucci's methods of work is given in a letter signed J.W.B.[2] that appeared in the *Numismatic Chronicle*, and the letter refers to the seal of the Duchy of Lancaster. To quote in full the writer's remarks: "Pistrucci's method is as follows:- He makes his design in wax or clay, imparting to his model the degree of finish he wishes finally to produce in metal: from this model a cast is made in plaster of Paris; which cast, having been hardened with drying oil, serves as a model from which an impression is very carefully taken in fine sand. From this a cast is made in iron; which iron cast Pistrucci employs as his die. It is obvious that by a very slight modification of his process, either a die or a punch is obtained; as it may be his object to produce a medal, or a seal, as in the case of the Duchy of Lancaster". The letter carries the heading of "Pistrucci's Invention" and I will return to the title aspect later in this history, but what it explains so well is this long complex procedure of Pistrucci's and clearly indicates that he was continuing to practise his own known method of work.

2   Numismatic Chronicle, 1838-39, Vol. 1, p59. It is very likely that the initials J. W. B stand for John William Burgon.

Chapter 2

Pistrucci, now almost fully recovered from his injury, had during the latter part of this time made some very fine bas-reliefs from his wax. These were seen by the well known cameo-merchant Domenico Desalief who gave him much praise at the Pistrucci home, and this obviously pleased Pistrucci senior so much that he began to take much more interest in Benedetto's progress. Benedetto felt that he ought to have a stone cutting machine and one was bought, made from a model of his own design.

Frederico decided his young son, who had now reached the age of fifteen, should have a new master and so the great Giuseppe Cerbara (1770-1856) was approached for a position. Benedetto's talents were most certainly recognised and he was offered a place. Yet to the absolute dismay of Pistrucci senior, his son refused this prestigious offer. Benedetto had declined to work under the great man because of the appalling conditions in which he was expected to operate. So a new master was sought and another famous name was approached; this time it was the eminent gem-engraver Nicola Morelli (1771-1838). Benedetto accepted a position with Morelli and very soon began to cut stones for him. He states in Billing: "In the space of eleven months, I made nine cameos for Morelli, amongst which were some both large and difficult; and in my leisure hours I made five for myself". Still waiting, as ever, to make further progress Benedetto attended the drawing academy at Campidoglio. As a result he achieved more success which in itself added greatly to his already fast increasing fame. However, this failed to go down well with Morelli who became quite jealous. He then said that Benedetto should spend all his time at his house, and so enough was enough for Benedetto who immediately packed his tools with his own machine and returned home. Pistrucci senior seeing his young son appear home unexpectedly was soon made aware of the situation and Benedetto was severely reprimanded. But again this brilliant young boy had his mind firmly resolved as to where his future would be, and Frederico was soon told that he was going to begin his career as a professor though he had yet to reach the age of sixteen! He already had plenty of commissions, and so he was able to give his family money for his keep, and to continue his work from the family home.

One of Pistrucci's first commissions came as a result of his earlier introduction to Domenico Desalief. This dealer, who was very highly regarded, gave Pistrucci a real antique cameo to be altered, simply because it had been so poorly done. It was in fact a very large sardonyx, and the subject was a warrior being crowned by a female figure; the whole cameo had been very badly cut and was even out of proportion. Pistrucci took two impressions of the piece, one before he begun his work, the other after the alteration. He also took a wax cast, using it to make a model of the new gem. Needless to say the new work of Pistrucci could not be faulted, and eventually it was to end up in the Imperial Cabinet of St. Petersburg. Many experts since have recognised it as an antique of the finest quality and even Denon, the Director of Medals in Paris, also made known his high opinion of it. Billing does in fact say the cameo was "as large as a man's hand".

Although there was much competition for Pistrucci, his classical style and brilliance had indeed by now been well noted and his clients included many well known collectors and other important people such as Desalief, Count Demidoff, Count Poniatowski, Blacas, General Bale (an Englishman living in Rome) and also a few cameo dealers. However, it has to be said at this point that during this period many contemporary cameos were being sold as genuine antiques. Even though Pistrucci had business transactions in his early days with dealers who would stoop to this sort of deception, he would never knowingly allow his cameos to be sold as antiques. Further more he even began to engrave on his cameos a special secret mark very well hidden in the design, and this was the Greek letter λ.

Pistrucci also carried out much work for the two main Roman dealers, one named Ignazio Vescovali and the other Angiolo Bonelli, and we shall see that the latter was to cause many problems for Pistrucci in the years ahead.

Pistrucci, still so young and as ever with the firm intention of progress, worked on and on. Yet during a rare social occasion he met a young lady named Barbara Folchi, then fourteen years of age and Pistrucci himself just sixteen. He very soon made up his mind he wanted to marry her, and two years later in 1802 they were married. Miss Folchi was the daughter of a well known, wealthy and respected Rome merchant, and Pistrucci senior was pleased to ask her father for her hand for Benedetto.

8

Benedetto and his wife quickly began a family with a girl named Victoria in 1803, his first son Vincenzio was born in 1804, and a daughter Catherine followed in 1806. In 1809 the family suffered a sad loss with the premature death of baby Elena, and in 1811 Camillo, another son, arrived. Four more children came later when the family were in England, and I will tell you more of these later in the history.

The reputation of Pistrucci was by now well established, and probably this resulted in his meeting Mr Rielli, Intendant General to the Grand-Duchess Baciocchi of Tuscany, sister of the Emperor Napoleon. Rielli was asked to request Pistrucci to make a portrait cameo of the Grand-Duchess, and at the same time she also ordered Rielli to place similar orders with Morelli (Pistrucci's old master) and also with Guiseppe Girometti, another fine engraver of that period. But a test was first to be carried out by all three artists, and a model done by Santarelli was to be copied by all three. However, only one month was given in which the work was to be completed, and Pistrucci was the last during the month to be given the model. In any event Pistrucci, as we know, did not like to copy another artist's work and it was to him quite obvious that both Morelli and Girometti were deliberately delaying the passing of the model over to him. So Pistrucci hunted around the junk shops of Rome and eventually found an old medal of the Grand-Duchess and although it was quite a poor example it enabled Pistrucci to begin his work. By now he was very short of time, and it is well worth quoting his own words from his part-autobiography in Billing: "From the time I began it, I never quitted it. I ate my dinner; like a labouring man, without ever sitting down; and, always sticking to my work, I finished it". In fact Pistrucci had done all his work on this magnificent cameo in just eight days! He delivered it on time as requested to the Intendant of the Treasury in Rome, and needless to say he won the test. Pistrucci was in fact given special permission to keep the model and make from it as many copies as he wished. Another model was sent to Pistrucci to begin his work for the Grand-Duchess but as usual he refused to copy, and eventually he was given a life sitting in Florence. The Grand-Duchess was so impressed with Pistrucci that he was provided with his own apartment within the Palace and given permission for his tools and machine to be sent from Rome since she wanted the work to be carried out in her Palace. When he had finished the portrait of the Grand Duchess she then asked him to engrave a cameo portrait of her daughter the Princess Napoleon; when this was finished he then cut one of her husband the Grand-Duke. While Pistrucci was doing this work many other notable people were aware of his presence within the Palace, and more than one wanted to have the expertise of the master. However, only one was given permission by the Grand-Duchess and this was the Marchesa Canami, daughter of the Spanish Ambassador. Pistrucci cut a portrait cameo for her. Finally Pistrucci made a minute onyx cameo of the Grand-Duchess and gave it to her as a present, in an ivory box; she was so pleased with it she had it set with large diamonds for a bracelet. Pistrucci's cameos in general very much pleased her, and as a result she told him that when the Emperor returned from the Russian campaign she would send him to the Court in Paris to make cameos of them both from life sittings. For parts of the year the Duchess would spend a little time in Pisa and generally Pistrucci went there also to continue his work, but on one such occasion they were forced to pack up and depart quickly because the English had disembarked a short distance off. They returned to Florence and Pistrucci resumed his work there, and as the situation worsened it looked very likely that Pistrucci might soon move yet again.

At this point it is worth referring to an incident affecting Pistrucci that had happened while he was working in Florence. Napoleon had made a decree that four Roman engravers of cameos should be sent to him, and they were to be professors of the Academy of St. Luke. Canova, who was the president, sent his chosen four, and Pistrucci was not one of them. This, of course, really upset Pistrucci and he never forgave Canova.

Soon after Pistrucci returned to Rome and he immediately went to see Canova and made his complaint in very forceful terms. Canova's answer was quite simply that professors were not made from people as young as Pistrucci and, as one would expect, this statement achieved nothing except to irritate Pistrucci even more. He replied in the words of Scipio "Ingrata-patria, nec mea ossa tenebis" which translated is "Ungrateful country, you shall not even have my bones". Pistrucci was very much a man of his word and kept his promise, for when he died he was buried in England.

Pistrucci by now was doing a great deal of work engraving cameos, and in 1808 this caused him a serious problem when as a result he almost lost his sight. It is well worth quoting his own words from Billing. "At the age of twenty-four, my great application to such minute objects as the finer parts of the cameos, and having just worked upon a stone which had a stratum of a fiery red colour, produced a weakness of the eyes so great that whenever I worked for half-an-hour my sight failed".

This illness was of course very serious, and became even more so when the leading physicians and surgeons of Rome could not bring about a cure. Pistrucci's family were in fact so concerned about his general attitude and depression that they seldom left him in the house alone.

Later a chemist by the name of Ricci visited Pistrucci at home, and seeing him so depressed gave him some medicine and invited him to go on a visit with him to his native place. He said the air there was so pure it had the power to restore the dead to life. Pistrucci's family encouraged him to go, and they left the next day. After a foolhardy trip on horses over mountainous terrain, encounters with French troops and with brigands, they finally arrived in Monte Reale at the home of Ricci's family. Here they found the country was under arms with French soldiers and they were repeatedly challenged; of course, they had no passports and so they experienced many problems.

The next day Pistrucci asked Ricci "if this was the care he had for my eyes, to bring me here to be shot in defending his country". Pistrucci had by this time decided enough was enough and the two of them left on horse-back the next day, intending to return to Rome via the city of Aquila. The return trip to Rome turned out to be fraught with danger; they were continually dodging the French soldiers and they had several near disasters with the gendarmes before finally getting through to Rome, and by this time at least the depression had gone from Pistrucci's mind; more importantly the serious problem of his eyesight was also apparently resolved.

Chapter 3

Angiolo Bonelli arrived back in Rome after a visit to England and gave Pistrucci a lot of work, he also suggested that Pistrucci should join him on a visit to England. Perhaps with the Canova incident still very fresh in his mind, Pistrucci was more than ready to seek fresh pastures, and so he agreed to accompany Bonelli to England.

Pistrucci made all necessary provision for his wife and family who were to remain in Italy, and left them sufficient funds to cover one year. He and Bonelli then set off for England. Their first stop was to be Perugia so that Benedetto could say goodbye to his brother Philip and this stop was indeed to prove really happy for Benedetto as Philip agreed to join them on the trip. The trio eventually arrived in Turin and Philip made it clear to his brother that he felt Bonelli was not an honourable man; furthermore he suggested that he ought not to go to England with him. However, Pistrucci would not during this period heed the warning, and the trio left for Paris where they arrived on 31 December 1814. By this time Philip's warning had sunk in and Benedetto as a result informed Bonelli that he and Philip were going to spend a few weeks in Paris, and that they would continue by themselves to London at a later date. Bonelli was furious and threatened Pistrucci that he would never set foot in London, to which Pistrucci replied by saying "to London I would come".

Benedetto and his brother remained in Paris, and Bonelli left for England on his own. Benedetto, whose name was well known in Paris to collectors and dealers, soon found plenty of work, but Philip got fed up with France and decided to return to Italy leaving Benedetto at work in Paris. But within a short while Napoleon, to the surprise of all, landed in France from the island of Elba and Pistrucci was in fact marooned for the hundred days. Even with a war going on the ever industrious Pistrucci worked on, and it was during this time that he saw Napoleon sitting in a garden nearby. As always he carried in his pocket his ball of wax, and with the opportunity presented out it came and very soon Napoleon unknowingly had been modelled in wax. Pistrucci's model (Plate 1) was possibly the last portrait of Napoleon done in Europe, and it was acknowledged as the best ever done of him.

The allies arrived in Paris, leading to the departure of Napoleon to

St. Helena, and it was then safe for Pistrucci to leave for London. He had a passport and to quote his own words: "I put in my pocket one hundred Napoleons in gold, and a letter of credit for twenty Louis. I took six cameos, done by myself in Italy, among which were some with a great deal of work; I took, likewise, a quantity of polished stones; in short everything I could want".

With his bags packed Pistrucci left for Calais arriving there with five French passengers who travelled on with him to Dover. They arrived late one Sunday afternoon in January 1815. Pistrucci was now very soon about to realise just how much trouble had been deliberately made for him by Bonelli, who had in fact arrived in Dover quite some time earlier and had most certainly bribed a few people and in general done everything he could to ensure that Pistrucci would not pass through customs and so on to London. After a long battle with the Dover officials Pistrucci eventually got help from James Millingen, a numismatist from London, whom he had met in Rome. Pistrucci wrote to him from Dover and as a result Millingen sent him a passport and also became security in respect of him. The next day he was able to leave for London, and arrived in the early hours of the following morning in Leicester Square where he found accommodation at Brunet's Hotel.

Pistrucci had brought with him several letters from friends for well known people in London, and one of these was to Charles König who held the position of Keeper of Minerals for the British Museum and another for Lord Fife. He managed to deliver these, and the one to König was to prove very fruitful for Pistrucci because it referred to him as "a most excellent cameo-cutter". From then on König took an obvious liking to Pistrucci and gave him much assistance in resolving all his problems, particularly some caused by Bonelli. During this period Pistrucci also suffered a serious chest illness, and again he was given much help by König who himself, along with the doctor he had provided, attended Pistrucci for the whole eighteen days it took to effect a cure. However, Pistrucci was not able to be free of chest problems during his many years in England, and some two years after the episode I have just described he was in need of further treatment. It is worth noting that at the time of this first illness Pistrucci had moved from Leicester Square into No 8 Panton Square.

With Pistrucci back to good health König then introduced him to Sir Joseph Banks, President of the Royal Society, and a person with many influential friends. He was also a botanist, and through König he had previously asked for Pistrucci to do a portrait of him. While he was actually engaged on this work Pistrucci was introduced to Richard Payne Knight, who was a very well known connoisseur of gems. What I will now relate to you about this chance meeting, which is described in detail in Billing, is I feel a fascinating episode and very indicative as to the true character of Pistrucci; it does in fact emphasise even more some of the greatness that Pistrucci has well and truly earned. Payne Knight had come to visit Sir Joseph Banks to show him a cameo fragment depicting a Flora (Plate 2). Pistrucci watched as it was passed to Banks, who examined it and praised it highly. At this point Pistrucci asked to see it and immediately said "That is my work". Knight, who spoke the Italian language fluently, fully understood what Pistrucci had said and was really angry at Pistrucci's statement. He replied "That is not true! Look at it well. You are mistaken!". He repeated this several times and then said "This is the finest Greek cameo in existence". Pistrucci in a sarcastic vein replied "I thank you, sir, for the compliments you pay me". Knight continued to argue and told Banks that further proof that the Flora was an antique lay in the wreath of flowers round the head; these were different from any modern ones, and the seed was missing. Banks responded most emphatically, saying "By God they are roses, and I am a botanist". Knight turned on Pistrucci again asking many questions about the Flora, but all were very convincingly answered, even to the point of Pistrucci showing Knight his own private mark which was discreetly placed in the hair of the Flora. Pistrucci had without doubt cut the cameo for Angiolo Bonelli some six years earlier, and the dealer had sold it to Knight for five hundred guineas! However, Banks was convinced that Pistrucci was nothing less than genuine, and Knight departed very much depressed at being made to look such a fool. The whole incident in fact only enhanced the reputation of Pistrucci, and Banks himself ordered a Flora cameo. Knight some time later visited Pistrucci at Panton Square and told him he had discussed with Bonelli all the circumstances now surrounding the Flora, but Bonelli insisted that Pistrucci was an imposter and a liar. So as a result of this visit Knight asked Pistrucci if he could give him better proof that he had actually cut the cameo. Although most indignant at this request Pistrucci said he would do this by cutting another Flora. Knight left and

14

Pistrucci began immediately on the new cameo. When Knight returned a few days later it was finished and was even better than the first! Knight presented no further problems.

With Banks now more than ever convinced that Pistrucci was not an imposter, and even more ready to recognise the ability that Pistrucci undoubtedly had, he asked Pistrucci to make a model in wax of George III. This was to be done the size of a sovereign, and Pistrucci was given a three-shilling piece by Marchant from which he was to copy. He was asked to work from Marchant because at that time it was not possible for Pistrucci to have a sitting with the King himself. Banks instructed Pistrucci to copy the Marchant bust exactly as to character, but he wanted Pistrucci to improve the style. The wax model was soon finished and, although Pistrucci was not entirely satisfied, it was approved by Banks, who as a result asked that a cameo be cut in stone from the wax. Pistrucci himself selected a red oriental jasper and the cameo was in due course completed for a payment of fifty guineas.

Banks continued to help Pistrucci and following the completion of the jasper cameo took him to meet Lord and Lady Spencer, a visit that was to prove of great value to Pistrucci and his eventual work for the Royal Mint. Lady Spencer spoke excellent Italian and immediately entered into conversation with Pistrucci; she showed him an oriental onyx, followed by a wax model of St. George by Marchant. She then said that her husband wanted Pistrucci to do a wax model of Marchant's St. George but she stressed that it must be of Greek style. This pleased Pistrucci immensely because this was already in his own mind, and had indeed been well implanted in his own style from his earlier apprenticeship and study. The naked figure of St. George would create the perfect Greek style in Pistrucci's eyes, and to present him in armour did not even bear to be thought of. Pistrucci eventually completed the wax model of St. George and the cameo followed in the normal way, to be used in fact by Lord Spencer with his insignia as a Knight of the Garter.

Chapter 4

In 1816 Banks provided the best introduction of all for Pistrucci, and it was to William Wellesley Pole (later Lord Maryborough) and Master of the Mint. Pole was a great friend of Banks and an extremely important man of the time; he had been appointed Master of the Mint on 6 July 1812, and at the Mint he was to undertake a total reorganisation of the staff and, later, the introduction of a new gold and silver coinage.

It is worth noting at this point, when Pistrucci was about to enter into the service of the Mint, that the problems and adversity he had already encountered during his life would continue, but as ever he battled on and succeeded. He had come to England with a reputation and skills that were of the highest order, so why should he yield to anyone from within the English establishment?

Banks had shown Pole the jasper cameo of George III that Pistrucci had cut for him, and as a result of this work Pole decided to engage Pistrucci to make the models for the dies of the new coinage. On 19 June 1816 Pole wrote to the Treasury[3]: "I have thought it desirable to employ Mr. Pistrucci, an artist of the greatest celebrity, whose works place him above all competition as a gem engraver, to make models for the dies of the new coinage and I request your Lordships to pay Mr. Pistrucci such remuneration as may be deemed necessary for his works. It is my intention that the models of Mr. Pistrucci should be engraved in jasper from which our engravers will work in steel, and the models will be deposited in the Royal Mint and remain there with the dies and Proof Impressions of the several coins"

Pistrucci could not officially be given the post of Chief Engraver on the grounds of his being an alien. So he was employed in the specially created position of an outside assistant to the engraving staff while Thomas Wyon continued as Chief Engraver.

3   Public Record Office, Mint 1/18, p358.

During the next six months Pistrucci cut three more effigies of George III in jasper and agate to be used for the three silver denominations needed urgently. Pistrucci suggested to Pole that his St. George would be most suitable for the reverse of the new gold coinage. Pole agreed and asked Pistrucci to cut a cameo in jasper for it, and when it was finished Wyon would be asked to copy it for the new gold coinage. Three magnificent jasper cameos survive in the Royal Mint Collection (Plates 3, 4 & 5). How wonderful it is that they have survived and that Pole's intentions came to fruition.

Shortly after the completion of the cameo Wyon died on 22 September 1817, and Pole decided that only Pistrucci was good enough to assume the duties of Chief Engraver. So Pistrucci took over the position, but not officially because of what I have previously explained. However, he was given the official residence within the Mint, and a salary of £500 per annum. The Mint records for the position were left blank, and remained so until 15 January 1828 when William Wyon was appointed Chief Engraver. He had previously held the position of second engraver under Pistrucci.

The reverse eventually recommended by Pole for the new sovereign (Plate 6 & 53) was the original he had asked Pistrucci to cut, and not the St. George engraved for Lord Spencer. In fact when Pistrucci had cut the Spencer cameo he had used as a model for St. George a waiter from Brunet's Hotel. So the new sovereign would on its obverse feature the King's head right, laureate with short hair; the tie loop with two ends, neck bare. Legend GEORGIUS III D:G: BRITANNIAR: REX F:D: the date is shown at the bottom of the coin under the truncation. The reverse features St. George with streamer flowing from helmet, mounted and slaying the Dragon with spear, the device being placed within the garter which replaces the legend and is inscribed HONI·SOIT·QUI·MAL·Y·PENSE. On the ground under the broken shaft of the spear are the tiny letters B.P. Pole's initials W.W.P have been cleverly placed on the buckle of the garter.

So the modern sovereign was born in 1817 and in appearance came entirely from the inventiveness and skill of Pistrucci. I am of the opinion that the reverse I have just described is the finest design ever to adorn any of our gold coinage. Indeed this supreme work of art has more than stood the test of time, and even today is still to be seen on our Queen's gold coins. One of Pistrucci's wax models for the sovereign was purchased at a sale in Rome by Captain Bruce Ingram, O.B.E and kindly given to the British Museum (Plate 53).

As ever one would expect Pistrucci's enemies to level criticism at the new sovereign, and of course at the engraver. The new obverse is perhaps not quite up to the quality of engraving that we would later see from Pistrucci, so I feel at this point it is relevant to refer to the sale catalogue of John G Murdoch[4] 1903-1904, and my first reference to this is Lot No 188. This item is a proof sovereign, the obverse of which simply displays the head of George III, and the reverse shows St. George slaying the dragon.

The coin comes from Pistrucci's own collection, and was sold with a note about the coin, that is also signed by him, which is well worth quoting in full: "Extremely rare proof of a sovereign, with head of George III, finished, but without lettering, the reverse is unfinished; my first work with the graving-tool, and struck without a collar. One may like to know that, when I did this work I had had no practice as yet in engraving on steel. After having engraved the puncheon, I had it tempered in its unfinished state, and a die executed from it. I had the surface of the die planed, and then struck this proof coin to see the effect of my work. After this, I made another puncheon, which I finished, feeling sure that my work was raised over a flat surface. One will see on this piece the marks of the wire-work design, which I drew to be sure of what I was doing, a thing I never had to do when engraving camei, an art in which I had more practice. It will be noticed further that the handle of the spear is shorter than on the current coins with the same St. George, and this I did so that the spear-handle should not pass over the horse, which did not seem tasteful to me. This piece is one of the most curious of my small series of proofs, and I value it highly because it is my first work which I saw struck from the presses of the Mint, &c. &c - B. PISTRUCCI.

4   Sale catalogue of Coins & Medals of J.G. Murdoch. 1903-4. Sotheby, pp18-19.

Lot No 190 from the same sale Catalogue is for two more Pistrucci proof sovereigns, and is also accompanied by a signed note from Pistrucci. It reads as follows: "Enclosed are two proofs in gold of the reverses of the sovereigns of H. M. George III. I may mention the history of these two proofs. The reader must be aware that this work was the first I did with the graving-tool, with out ever having seen anybody engraving in steel; it is therefore not one of my best, but one should bear in mind that it requires ten years practice to do such work well. I did it to satisfy Mr. Pole, who ordered it. These proofs were struck from a die which had passed four times through the fire, and got worse each time, the action of the first spoiling the edges, and I am only surprised that they are as good after so many experiments. I had these proofs made, as I wanted to see the effect of the hand holding the bridle, as, after having completed my work from the model, they made me change the hand, which was at first showing a portion of the arm, to what is now seen on the current coins. These are of the highest rarity and unique". Presented by Mr. Pole. B. PISTRUCCI.

I feel that these two notes tell us much about Pistrucci, and they not only illustrate his ability as an engraver, but also show him to be a man of real integrity. By his own admission he had never used a graving-tool before, and had no previous experience of engraving steel. Yet in spite of this he was confident and brave enough to produce what I believe was an excellent new coinage for George III, and I do not think any further comment is necessary. My final point arising from the notes is his comment in the second note that reads: "it requires ten years practice to do such work well". He was of course, referring not only to the use of the graving-tool but also to working in steel. From this one can only conclude that Pistrucci was not merely a very quick learner, but also a superb one, because less than four years on he produced the magnificent laureate bust for George IV.

Later in 1817, during October, a half-sovereign was introduced and this was similar to the sovereign, but with a very different reverse. It featured an angular shield, surmounted by the royal crown, bearing the Ensigns Armorial of the United Kingdom. The new gold coinage was to be completed with a double-sovereign and a five-pound piece (Plates 7 & 8) but these were in fact only struck as proof coins and only after the death of the King. They bear the date of 1820 and are indeed extremely rare, because only sixty specimens of the double-sovereign were struck, and for the larger denomination only around twenty five pieces. In my opinion they are without equal in any of our modern gold coinage, and they clearly indicate the skill that Pistrucci had developed as a die engraver, and more than refute the earlier criticism levelled at him when the sovereign was introduced. The five-pound obverse features the large laureate bust of the King facing right, neck bare with PISTRUCCI immediately below the truncation, and the date. The legend reads GEORGIUS III D: G: BRITANNIAR: REX F: D. The reverse displays Pistrucci's magnificent St. George slaying the Dragon, and the full name of PISTRUCCI is again shown this time just below the exergue line on the left. The double-sovereign is very similar to the larger coin except that the obverse has the small laureate bust of the King and does not carry Pistrucci's name. The reverse again displays St. George slaying the Dragon with the initials B.P. shown just below the exergue line in the more normal position on the right. Both coins are plain edged and carry the same lettered edge that reads DECUS ET TUTAMEN ANNO REGNI LX, and also shown on both reverses close to the broken spear shaft are the initials W.W.P. Perhaps Pole was endorsing in this way his support for Pistrucci to place his name on his own work? One cannot leave the coinage of George III without special reference to the five shilling piece (Plate 9). This wonderful coin produced by Pistrucci and introduced in October 1818 was indeed magnificent, and a period of nearly seventy years had elapsed since a silver crown of its size had last been struck. This large silver coin featured on its obverse the large laureate bust of the King facing right, the neck bare and PISTRUCCI written in full below the truncation, the date at the bottom, and the legend surrounding the bust. The reverse displays Pistrucci's St. George slaying the Dragon and below the exergue line once again the name PISTRUCCI appears in full, and the initials of the Master W.W.P are once more placed on the buckle of the garter. The device placed within the garter that carries the inscription HONI·SOIT·QUI·MAL·Y·PENSE. These coins were given special treatment in their production at the mint, and some were in fact to have a lettered edge inscription. Special collars were made that would carry the usual inscription, and all the coins were handled with great care even though they were currency pieces. They were struck as medals were by a series of graduated blows to ensure a better end result, whereas the normal coin at that time would have been struck by only one blow. The finished coin was eventually wrapped in soft paper for its delivery to the banks and other sources, and with its delivery went an instruction from the Mint that these coins were not to be roughly handled, they would then reach their clients in pristine condition. This magnificent silver crown attracted much criticism from the Press, and from other critics, who in the main were members of the Wyon family, and were as always ready to condemn the work of Pistrucci. In respect of the silver crown the criticism levelled by those mentioned was based on the fact that not only was the name of PISTRUCCI on the coin, but also the Master's initials. I have already made clear my opinion on the silver crown; and perhaps it should also be noted that when Pistrucci's involvement with the coinage ceased in 1824, a period of more than twenty years passed before the Mint found it necessary to strike crowns again.

Aside from all the work on the coins that I have mentioned for the new coinage, Pistrucci also carried out many repairs on dies and other items during this same period from 1 January 1817 until 1 December 1817. The Mint records[5] for this period have a number of entries relating to the repair work, and the account also lists the following larger items, £525 for the engraving of the silver Crown, for the first George and the reverse of the sovereign £315, for engraving the half-crown now in use £84. The account also lists two sums of money paid to Pistrucci for a trip he made with Pole to Paris to study French works of art and also to discuss designs. Pistrucci received £55 for the journey to Paris, and £32-12s for coaches to and from the Mint. The total figure for the above year was £1322-5s-6d and I am quite sure Pistrucci really earned every penny of it, and in fact he was known many times to have actually worked more than eighteen hours a day. Another very important outcome of the visit to Paris was that Pistrucci bought for himself an early reducing[6] or copying machine, and this proved to be a great success at the Mint because it enabled the engraver to save a lot of time and bypass much laborious hand work. It is very likely Pistrucci would have instructed his staff on the use of the new machine, and William Wyon later used a similar machine extensively for the master dies of Queen Victoria's first coinage. The Mint was so impressed with this new and revolutionary machine that later in 1824 they ordered a new one for

5   Public Record Office, Mint 3/20
6   Numismatic Chronicle Vol. II, pp311-317. "Matthew Bolton and the Reducing Machine" by J. G. Pollard.

21

themselves from Paris at a cost of 4000 francs, and this was indeed money well spent because its introduction had already allowed considerable cost savings to be made.

After a very productive year that required a great effort from Pistrucci he once again became ill and it was necessary for him to write to the doctor who attended him before. The letter[7] (see Plate 10) in translation reads:

Mr. Pistrucci pays his compliments to Dr Tobler and although he knows how inconvenient it is for him to be asked to come to visit him in such a far-away place, in spite of this he is forced by necessity to ask this favour of the doctor as the writer of this letter has been very ill for more than a week with a chest and head chill which gave him a fever for a few days, and he does not want to be without the famous hand of that doctor which healed him before. Therefore, the writer is waiting on his convenience also because he thinks it necessary to consult him about his wife.

3 March 1818 Apartment 4 Royal Mint.

The letter was originally sent folded and the signature of Pistrucci was placed separately on the inside of the written letter.

I was pleased to acquire this hand-written letter in 1987, and it is interesting to note that the water-mark clearly indicates the maker as W. TURNER & SON with the date of 1814.

---

7   Author's collection.

Chapter 5

Pistrucci was expected to carry out other work in his position of Chief Engraver, and part of his terms of employment was to produce any medals needed by the Government. During this, the early part of his career at the Mint, he received two very important commissions for medals. The first was for a medal to mark the occasion of the purchase by the Government of the Elgin Marbles for the British Museum. This commission very likely came about because of his friend William Richard Hamilton, who was then Under Secretary for Foreign Affairs, and also Lord Elgin's private secretary.

He had also arranged the first public exhibition of the Marbles in London in 1808. The wax models of the medal are preserved in the Museo Della Zecca in Rome, and they show the date of 1817-1820 for the proposed medal. The later King, George IV, was at this time Prince Regent, and for several years he had shown such interest in the Marbles that perhaps it was he who was instrumental in giving Pistrucci the commission.

The second commission, and by far the more important, was for a medal to commemorate Waterloo and the defeat of Napoleon in the long war with France. The proposal for the medal was in fact made by the Prince Regent as early as 1816.

Apart from eventually bringing supreme fame to Pistrucci, the commission of the Waterloo Medal caused him countless problems before it was finished, and so it is important that they are detailed in this history of the Italian engraver. They fully endorse Pistrucci's stubbornness and will to succeed. As was the custom in those days the Royal Academy was invited to submit a design for the medal, and eventually a design by John Flaxman the celebrated sculptor was submitted. Pistrucci was asked to work from it but as always he refused to copy the work of another artist, much to the annoyance of the Royal Academy. As a result of this Pole asked Pistrucci to submit his own design, and within twenty four hours he produced wax models for the Prince Regent. These were instantly recognised as truly magnificent works of art, and the Prince was lavish with his praise for these wonderful Pistrucci waxes. A commission was imminent.

A letter from Treasury Chambers dated 20 August 1819 informed Pole that his request to employ Pistrucci for the purpose of engraving the Waterloo Medal was granted, and the minute[8] that followed this read, "In pursuance of the above authority the Master of the Mint was pleased to enter into an agreement with Mr. Pistrucci for the execution of the Waterloo Medal at the price of £2400. The said sum to be paid to Mr. Pistrucci by imprests from time to time until the work is completed". At this stage it is important to point out that as a result of this minute Pistrucci had in fact entered into a private arrangement with Pole, but Pole had, of course, acted on Treasury authority. Another important factor was that the extra money this commission brought Pistrucci would enable him to bring his beloved family to England, and at this point his Mint salary was not enough for him to bring this about. Pole had promised an early advance of £2000 in respect of the Waterloo Medal commission, and this allowed him at last to reunite with his family.

A further problem presented itself when the Prince Regent sent Pistrucci a portrait of himself by the Court painter Sir Thomas Lawrence, and the request with it asked Pistrucci to copy it, along with the other three sovereigns, for the obverse of the new Waterloo Medal. Pistrucci, of course, would have none of it, for he had never yet condescended to copy another artist's work. A few weeks later Pole visited Pistrucci to see what progress had been made, and he was dismayed to find nothing had been done. He was even more upset when he discovered the Lawrence portrait had been deposited against a wall, and also with its face to the wall. Although threatened with dismissal Pistrucci, as he had done many times past, still flatly refused to copy the Lawrence portrait. Eventually he was given several life-sittings from the Prince Regent. However, once again because he had rightly insisted on expressing his own skills he gave offence to several important people, and as on similar past occasions they caused him to bear the brunt of much unfair criticism. His critics, though, were blind to the brilliance and forethought that occupied the great engraver's mind, for he made more than full use of the life sittings granted by the Prince Regent. He went on to use the waxes he had created from the sittings not only for the Waterloo Medal, but also for the Coronation Medal for George IV, and then for the King's new coinage. How emphatically they were to prove his point, for all are superb examples of his outstanding engraving ability.

8   Public Record Office, Mint 1/20, p300. The sum mentioned in this minute later became £3500

The Waterloo Medal is in my opinion the finest piece of intaglio engraving ever seen. This masterpiece with its brilliant combination of allegorical and classical design enables Pistrucci to be described as possibly the greatest engraver ever, and certainly the modern era has produced no one to equal him. The medal was Pistrucci's own design, and its actual size if struck would have been 140 millimetres; no medal of this kind and size had ever been struck before. The Napoleon medals by Andrieu although a similar size were from dies formed only for the striking of single medals, and in soft metal. The design content of them bore no comparison with the Waterloo Medal and Pistrucci himself estimated that the work necessary for engraving the Waterloo Medal equalled that of thirty ordinary size medals. Before he could begin his work it was necessary for him to select the steel blocks upon which the matrices would be engraved, and eventually he chose two 20lb blocks of the highest quality for these wonderful matrices (Plate 11). (Plate 57) shows Tom Pistrucci at the Royal Mint in 1986 admiring the matrices.

The obverse of the Waterloo Medal is an allegory of peace except for the centre, which contains the busts in profile of the four allied Sovereigns. Around this group of portraits Apollo in his chariot is restoring the day, Iris with her rainbow and Zephyr follow the chariot of the sun in succession, scattering flowers as the emblem of peace; the chariot is seen approaching the constellation Gemini that appears as usual in the form of a pair of youths, and is indicating the month in which the great contest took place. Castor and Pollux each armed with a spear denote the apotheosis of Wellington and Blucher. Themis, the goddess of Justice, appears on earth, as in the golden age; she is placed in front of the central busts to indicate that justice is greater than power, and a palm tree appears near her head; with some branches in one hand she is prepared to reward virtue, but in the other hand a sword is grasped ready to punish crime. Behind the busts the figure of Power is personified by a muscular bearded man armed with a club and seated under an oak tree. Beneath Themis the Fates appear and indicate that in the future human action will be controlled by justice alone, and these actions and passions are represented by the Furies which are cleverly placed beneath the figure of Power, and are thus subject to its influence. At the bottom of this side of the medal the figure of Night is introduced, the mother of the Fates, who is fleeing from Apollo.

The reverse features at its centre the mounted figures of Wellington and Blücher in the same classical style that Pistrucci introduced with his famous St. George and Dragon design used for the sovereign. Wellington the victor is galloping in front, and the veteran Blücher is charging along at the rear to aid his companion and complete the destruction of the enemy. Between the two is placed the flying figure of Victory guiding their horses to the battle. On the outer edge and forming a border round the central group is a composition of figures; they represent the Giants, and have been struck down by Jupiter above, tumbling downwards in total confusion to indicate the confusion of the defeated enemy. The Giants in all number nineteen, symbolising the nineteen years of the war. Pistrucci's original wax models of the medal have survived and are kept at the Museo Della Zecca at Rome; they indicate that the medal was to have had an inscription on both sides (Plates 12 &13).

So with Pistrucci's financial position now much more secure as a result of the Waterloo Medal he continued with his efforts on the coinage dies, and his other everyday work at the Mint. For the coinage work he was greatly assisted by the appointment of Jean Baptiste Merlen, a French engraver who had been especially asked for by Pistrucci because at that time the engraving staff were well below strength. Merlen went on in fact to cut nearly all the new coin reverses till 1844.

Pistrucci's next official duty was the medal for the coronation of George IV, and this certainly caused him a few problems. First he had to reproduce the unusual toupee worn by the King; then when the proofs were shown to the King he would not accept Pistrucci's reverse. He said it was not correct because he had been placed on the same level as the allegorical figures of England, Scotland and Ireland! A very worried Master reported the complaint to Pistrucci, and also stressed that very little time remained before the medal would be wanted. Pistrucci replied almost immediately saying "I shall elevate His Majesty". He then perpendicularly cut the die in two, just at the King's foot, then slightly raised one piece above the other thus raising that part of the platform under the throne above the other part. He then continued the under line of the platform to make the whole piece level. By this simple but quick alteration he had done what the King requested, and had raised him to a position above his subjects. The problem had been overcome, and the King accepted Pistrucci's final work (Plate 14). Pistrucci was paid £500 for his work on the coronation medal, although he had earlier requested a much larger fee of £1200.

The new coinage was becoming an urgent requirement and so Pistrucci returned to his work of its preparation, and all the obverses of the new coinage issued in 1821 were cut by him using the same laureate head bust as he had used for the coronation medal. The new sovereign (Plate 15) features on its reverse a changed version of St. George slaying the Dragon; St. George is seen with a sword in his hand instead of the shivered lance, the streamer is missing from the rear of the helmet, and gone also is the garter. The new silver coinage contained yet another Pistrucci gem by the introduction once more of a currency crown (Plate 16). The obverse carries the magnificent laureate bust of the King to the left, the reverse displays St. George slaying the Dragon, and the coin has a lettered edge. However, this time Pistrucci does not feature his name in full, and only his initials B.P. are shown on both obverse and reverse. The coin was described by Vivant Denon, director of the French Mint, as the handsomest coin in Europe.

During 1821 the King made official visits to both Ireland and Hanover, and medals were proposed for both visits. Pistrucci, it seems, carried out considerable work in respect of both medals, and four of his wax impressions for the Irish medal survive in Rome, and also one similar wax for the Hanover visit. However, Pistrucci again refused to copy a Chantrey bust for the Irish medal, and as a result I do not believe either medal was eventually commissioned.

Much happened during 1823 that would greatly affect the career of Pistrucci, beginning in August of that year when the Master of the Mint William Wellesley Pole resigned. As a token of respect and gratitude for Pole the officers of the Mint commissioned Pistrucci to engrave a medal (Plate 45) in his honour, and Pole was later presented with eight of these medals in gold; he also received twenty in the cheaper metals of silver and bronze. The obverse of the medal simply features the bust of Pole facing right, and the reverse displays in very small Latin letters the inscription which translated reads: In honour of that remarkable man, William Wellesley Pole, Baron Maryborough, for nine years Master of the Mint, who did not only restore the British coinage to its original splendour, but made it new and more beautiful. He organised the despatch of coins into all parts of the country with such skill that almost simultaneously everywhere the old money passed into disuse, and the new was swiftly brought into public use. The moneyers caused this medal, a memorial of their regard and friendship, to be struck at the Royal Mint in London, 1823. The obverse die (Plate 46) for the Pole medal has survived and is in the Royal Mint collection, and a lead trial striking (Plate 47) for the obverse of the same medal also still exists in the Fitzwilliam Museum collection.

The resignation of Pole meant that Pistrucci lost not only his Chief but also a good friend and admirer. However, Pole had gone and he was replaced by Thomas Wallace as the new Master. Pistrucci continued as the principal engraver, and later in 1823 the new two-pound piece was issued. It had a similar reverse to that of the sovereign except that the streamer was re-introduced at the rear of the helmet. The obverse displays a new bust engraved by Merlen from a bust by Sir Francis Chantrey, and this was brought about because once again Pistrucci had refused to copy another artist's work. Pistrucci had in effect almost withdrawn his services by refusing to re-produce the Chantrey bust, but in spite of more insinuations and harassment by Mint officials he kept his position and salary of £500. Wyon also continued as second engraver with a salary of £200.

In effect Pistrucci had very little to do with the coinage after the Chantrey refusal, and the new coinage for George IV in 1825 was carried out completely by Merlen and Wyon. Pistrucci continued to be busy at the Mint during this period, and again asked the Mint for a proper appointment and recognition as Chief-Engraver, but again his request fell on deaf ears.

Chapter 6

The year of 1825 does I feel contribute a good deal to the history of Pistrucci, and it in fact brought to the Mint the promising young German Carl Friedrich Voigt. Part of Pistrucci's duties was the teaching of his assistants and any chosen pupils, and earlier I have mentioned Merlen and William Wyon both of whom were for a considerable time assistants under Pistrucci. Their achievements as engravers are well known, but Voigt of the three is probably to us the least known. But he is without a doubt important to the Pistrucci history. He came to Pistrucci at the age of 25 but he already had an excellent start to his career behind him, beginning when he was accepted as an apprentice by the German engraver and goldsmith Vollgold. He was taught to model with wax by Leonard Posch, and from 1820 to 1825 he worked at the medal and coin establishment of G.Loos. In his last year with Loos he received the academic prize in modelling from life and consequently received a scholarship. In November 1825 Voigt left Ostende to go to the London Mint, and in his own[18] words he said "to see the best Mint in the world". He left with a recommendation from the director of the Mint in Utrecht for Pistrucci, and the purpose of the visit was to cut the dies for the new coinage of Columbia. However, this country later decided to cut their own coinage, and Voigt shortly after received a very attractive offer to go to Columbia. Meantime Voigt decided he would continue to London. His arrival at the Mint was not at all pleasant as the money which had been promised him by the Prussian ministry had failed to arrive. He also found that Pistrucci was not at the Mint. Eventually Pistrucci returned and Voigt was able to begin his work at the Mint. The young German had brought with him a medal of Lord Eldon that he had engraved in Rome. The medal gained for him general approval, and Pistrucci soon liked his new arrival and his attitude towards learning.

Voigt stayed working under Pistrucci for around a year, and during this time he undoubtedly benefited much from the tuition Pistrucci had given him. In fact Voigt himself said "my stay with him was of great advantage for me. It was in his office that I made my first work in stone".

18   Allgemeines Lexikon de bildenden Künstler, begrundet von Ulrich Thieme und Felix Becker, Leipzig 1929.

Later in 1826 I am sure Voigt showed his appreciation by the excellent bronze uniface portrait medallic plaque he engraved of Pistrucci (Plate 17). The plaque is 86 millimetres and features the very young looking Pistrucci bust right, with the inscription BENEDETTO PISTRUCCI STEIN-UND STEMPELSCHNEIDER (Benedetto Pistrucci, stone and gem cutter). The plaque is signed C. Voigt followed by the date 1826 below the truncation. This is a fine example and was purchased at the Glendinings sale of Historical Medals in London on 22nd November 1989 by the Royal Mint, and it is a very important portrait of Pistrucci who was at that time forty two years of age. I know of only two of these plaques and they must be considered of the highest rarity: and the second (Plate 18) only appeared quite recently this year. It is a beautiful crisp casting and is as struck; it measures 86 millimetres and is cast in gilt bronze with a magnificent gilt frame that has a suspension loop at the top. The provenance of the plaque is indeed remarkable and it comes from the prestigious cabinet of the Grand Ducal Court of Baden, and the Grand Duke's original label is still attached. The inventory drawn up by Karl Koelitz in 1883 shows works of art, put together as a private Kunstkammer collection by the Grand Duke Friedrich I (1826-1907) after 1879 in the rooms of the former Grand Ducal Naturalienkabinet in the Residenzschloss, Karlsruhe. The inventory drawn up by the gallery inspector Richter shows the works of art described by Koelitz and brought to the Neues Schloss Baden-Baden after the property division of the Grand Ducal House and State of Baden in 1919.

Voigt left the Mint in 1826 and travelled via Paris and Milan to Rome and it is from this point on that some most interesting connections were made by Voigt. They seem very much to link back to Pistrucci, and it is most likely that he was involved, certainly in the case of Thorwaldsen who as we shall see enjoyed an association with Pistrucci. The stop in Rome brought about his introduction to the great gem cutter Girometti and by him he was given much tuition and advice on the engraving of cameos. In return he gave similar advice to Girometti about the engraving of steel dies. Voigt went on to cut some fine miniatures in onyx, all of which were masterly executed. Then through Schadow a commission was arranged for him to cut for the Crown Princess Elizabeth of Prussia a collar in carnelian that featured the myth of Cupid and Psyche. This work got the young German very well known, and to his great advantage it encouraged Albert Thorwaldsen to take him on.

Voigt was given a commission arranged by Thorwaldsen to engrave the prize medal of the Academia Tiberina, and for this work he was made a member of the Academia. Following this he was invited by the Royal Mint of Berlin to be one of the applicants for the production of coin dies with the portrait of the King. Voigt's entry won the prize and as a result he was well on his way to the great success he eventually attained. After his long but very advantageous stay in Rome he then in 1829 travelled on to Munich, where King Ludwig I appointed him Chief Engraver and First Medallist of the Mint.

Voigt's success I am sure was influenced by the work he carried out for the Crown Princess Elizabeth of Prussia. She was the sister of Ludwig I, and the daughter of King Maximilian I. Elizabeth's husband the Crown Prince Friedrich Wilhelm succeeded his father in June 1840, and so it seems that Voigt's success can be largely attributed to the Crown Princess and her husband. I feel that it would not be unreasonable to suggest that the second Voigt plaque of Pistrucci was possibly Voigt's own, and that he may have used it to demonstrate his ability and skill to the Crown Prince and his wife. From there it very likely found its way into the Baden cabinet.

At Munich Voigt was engaged in cutting the dies for the coinage of Greece of King Otho, and also the medals of that King. For the Bavarian coinage of King Ludwig I he cut many dies from 1829 onwards, and he went on to cut dies for King Maximilian and also King Ludwig II. He engraved dies for some of the Papal currency of Pope Pius VIII (Bologna and Roma 1830) and also some for Pius IX.

Some of his other notable achievements were the great gold medal with the portrait of Duke Maximilian in Bavaria, the prize medal of the Kurhessische Academy in Havana with the portrait of Michelangelo and a medal for Bogota with the statue of Simon Bolivar made by Tenerani. On the reverse the abolition of slavery after a relief of the existing monument for Baron of Kreittmayr (1845). One of his last commissions was the die for the peace-coin of 1871.

During his career Voigt received many awards and numerous academies honoured him, including those of Munich and Rome. He was made a Knight of the Order of St. Michael and of Our Redeemer of Greece.

Voigt's career ranks high in the field of engravers, and the influence of both Pistrucci and Thorwaldsen is unmistakable in his work, especially in its mythological and allegorical forms.

It is of particular interest to note that, as in the case of Pistrucci, Voigt engraved a medal of Thorwaldsen, and it was struck in 1837. The obverse features the bust of Thorwaldsen and his name, and on the reverse his celebrated group of Erato and Cupid. It seems that again Voigt was showing his appreciation of a good master.

This part of the Pistrucci history can be very appropriately concluded by quoting some of Pistrucci's own words when being chided by some of his friends who felt very strongly that he should not convey his mode of working, or pass on information, to all engravers who were under him. Pistrucci replied to them: "I feel certain to surpass them all; therefore, the higher any one of them stands, he only elevates me".

In 1827 George Tierney M.P was appointed the new Master, and was faced with a further request by Pistrucci, but by this time Pistrucci's official payments had reached £8500. Tierney said that they must stop, and on 15 January 1828 he appointed William Wyon as Chief Engraver and Pistrucci as Chief Medallist. Both men were given a salary of £350 each per year. In the case of Pistrucci's salary the last £50 of it was conditional on his training a pupil to advance the medallic art in England. In turn Pistrucci named his son Camillo, and then another son Raphael, but since neither met the requirement of the Mint on 1 January 1831 the payment was stopped.

So after the continued period of agitation by the Mint and others Pistrucci finally had to stand aside for Wyon, but he was not too much dismayed because in achieving the position of Chief Medallist he had elevated himself considerably in the eyes of his Roman friends, and he was also at last officially recognised in the Mint records. He also still retained his house at the Mint, and of course he very much wanted to finish the Waterloo Medal. The many problems of the past in the main presented by officials of the Mint and the uncertainty they caused him had made him unwilling to finish the medal, which he vowed he would not complete until his position was recognised and the Mint acknowledged his work.

A decision made by Pistrucci that centred around the problems I have described was to send his family back to Rome and this brought him much grief because he loved them so much. But the reason for this was that he was literally in a war with officials of the Mint, and to quote his own words he would be more at liberty "to carry on the war" if they were out of it. Apart from this they would be with friends and relations, and they could also be educated and supported much more economically. So his wife and family left for Rome in 1824 but his eldest son Camillo stayed on at the Mint with his father, and he was soon able to draw and model really well. Eventually when he was eighteen Pistrucci sent him to Rome with a letter for Albert Thorwaldsen who gave him instruction, and from there he progressed to one of the top glyptic positions under the Pope's Government. His job was to supervise the restoration of all the antique statues which were constantly being discovered in Rome, and in fact some of these great restorations he actually carried out himself.

Aside from official commissions Pistrucci now divided his work between the Waterloo Medal and gems for private clients. His new position allowed him to do this, and he was not short of commissions from private sources. His clients included the Duke of Wellington, Lord Lauderdale, Lord and Lady Spencer, Sir Joseph Banks and W.R Hamilton, to name but a few.

Pistrucci's cameos are very rare, and so far less than ninety are known, and the majority of these are in National Museum collections, three are in the Royal Mint Collection, and only a few are in private collections. These cameos are really exquisite and magnificent works of art, and most carry the great engraver's signature. When he cut cameos Pistrucci was known to have used several different types of gem-stones, but I think his favourite must have been the sardonyx. This was a stone where the white layers, or layer, alternated with red, brown, black or orange-red carnelian colours. These stones enabled Pistrucci to select a different colour for perhaps three different parts of his chosen subject. This would of course vary depending on the number of strata in the chosen stone. Invariably the stones he used would be from a single stratum to five strata.

One should remember that many of his cameos were cut on stones that were often less than six millimetres in thickness, and so for a stone containing say four strata, one could imagine the degree of accuracy needed by Pistrucci when he sought to find the limit of each layer for the particular part of his design.

I find it near impossible to describe the skill needed to create such exquisite beauty from such small gems that Pistrucci used, and to appreciate this they have to be seen in reality. In general they are very rare.

At this juncture it is worth mentioning several cameos that Pistrucci cut, and the large fees he was able to command for his work: a head of Medusa in jasper 200 guineas, Young Bacchus in carnelian/onyx 300 guineas, Leda and the Swan in onyx 200 guineas, Force subdued by Love and Beauty in sardonyx 200 guineas, a large Minerva (nearly 4 inches) in oriental chalcedony onyx 500 guineas, the Order of St. Andrew, the figure standing behind the Cross with the motto of the order in sardonyx 350 guineas, a copy of the Liris Bronze 250 guineas, Augustus and Livia in sapphirine 800 guineas. These prices clearly indicate that Pistrucci not only had very wealthy clients but that they were also prepared to pay large sums for his work.

Pistrucci resumed his work on the Waterloo Medal, and also continued with his duties as Chief Medallist, and he produced several medals in the next five or so years. In 1824 he engraved the Laudatory Medal of George IV, and this was a speculative venture by the Court Jewellers Messrs Rundell, Bridge and Rundell. The large medal did not sell and in fact most were melted. The next Pistrucci medal came in 1826 which was a bronze medal of 46 millimetres by W.J Taylor after B. Pistrucci (Plate 19) to mark the death of Taylor Combe, Keeper of Coins at the British Museum. In 1827 Pistrucci was commissioned by Thomas Hamlet to make a large medal of the Duke of York (Plate 20) and he also produced a smaller version of this same medal that was less than half an inch in diameter; they were in gold and gilt. These tiny medals were very popular with the King's friends and were often worn in rings. When one considers that the Waterloo Medal was 140 millimetres and this minute medal of the Duke of York less than half an inch, Pistrucci had in effect produced both the largest and smallest medals ever executed.

Chapter 7

In 1825 Pistrucci was approached by the Royal Humane Society regarding work for the Fothergillian Medal; this medal is a relatively unknown one of Pistrucci's.

A will of Dr Anthony Fothergill dated 7 September 1810 left the Royal Humane Society £500, and this sum was to be used for an annual or biennial medal for the best essay or discovery on the following subjects:
1. The prevention of shipwreck.
2. The preservation of shipwrecked Mariners or other circumstances left to the Society's discretion.

Although Fothergill died in 1813 the bequest was not received until 1821, and then it took another three years before in November 1824 Messrs Rundell, Bridge and Rundell received a letter from James Bandinall of the Royal Humane Society. The letter asked if two complete dies the size of the Coronation Medal, and three proofs, one in each metal of gold, silver and copper, could be supplied to the Society. The Society would provide the metal, and including all expenses the fee offered was 100 guineas. The details of the medal were listed as follows: the obverse would feature the bust of Fothergill with an inscription, and the reverse was to be Leucothea and Ulysses from Homer's Odyssey, again with an appropriate inscription. Rundell Bridge replied to this letter saying it was not possible to meet these requirements for 100 guineas. Bandinall then visited Rundell Bridge and explained that because of the death of Thomas Wyon Jnr the society felt that the execution of the work might not produce the degree of excellence required unless they could commission Mr. Pistrucci. Bandinall was told that Pistrucci's fees might well be around 300 guineas.

Eventually the Royal Humane Society decided to bypass Rundell Bridge and go direct to Pistrucci. He was asked to submit an estimate for the replacement of the original Society dies that were engraved by Lewis Pingo in 1775, and also for a new design for the Fothergill Medal. Pistrucci was also asked to include the striking of three proof medals one in gold, one in silver and one in copper. He was also asked to state the time needed for his work, and the society gave notice that they would require him to complete any order given within three months from when he received the order.

Pistrucci replied by letter to the Society agreeing to meet all their requests regarding the existing dies, and also to provide designs of his own for a new medal. His total cost for all the work would by 135 guineas, and he asked the Society if he could make alterations to the dies if he felt he was able to improve them, especially that of the figure of the young boy.

The Royal Humane Society considered Pistrucci's estimate for all their work to be most reasonable. After some time Pistrucci was asked to proceed, although the time schedule took rather longer than expected due to various changes in both the committee and its officers. However, the business relating to the existing medal went on well, but meantime the Society acquired a new Secretary, Berkeley Westropp. He wrote to Pistrucci on August 24 1830 requesting a proof of the medal if the dies were finished. Pistrucci had completed the work and Mint records show that the Royal Humane Society gave Pistrucci eight orders for medals during the period from March 1831 until November 1837, resulting in 145 medals being supplied.

The new Fothergill Medal had still not been finished by 1830. Much debate and argument appears to have occurred over the long period that followed, and we also know that Pistrucci himself complained several times to the Society about the continued delays relating to his final instructions. Then finally in 1837 wax models by Pistrucci were examined by the Society, and it was agreed by the committee that Pistrucci be written to for his terms, and if acceptable he should be employed. But it appears that one individual, Secretary Westropp, made a private decision of his own to replace Pistrucci with another artist, Scipio Clint. New designs were produced by Clint in February 1838 and were accepted, and Westropp took these to the Mint to discuss with Pistrucci, and the explosive result was exactly that which could have been predicted. This confrontation caused by such stupidity can be best explained if I quote in full the account of it from an excellent paper by Mark Jones entitled *The Fothergillian Medal* published in *The British Numismatic Journal* 1984[9].

9   The British Numismatic Journal 1984, pp248-62. The Fothergillian Medal by Mark Jones.

One must, of course, realise though that it was prepared by Westropp himself, yet I feel it does very much illustrate many of Pistrucci's real and genuine qualities. I quote:

The account laid before the Fothergillian Sub-committee on 26 and 28 March. "The Secretary of the Royal Humane Society called on Mr. Pistrucci at the Royal Mint on Monday the 19 last with a model of a design for the Fothergillian Medal, furnished by Mr. Clint Jnr and adopted by the Sub-committee to whom that duty was entrusted.

"The Secretary was received by Mr. Pistrucci in a public workshop in the Mint, and when the model was laid before him he disapproved of it with a look of contemptuous scorn, observing - "that it might well do enough for the fifteenth century, or for a picture; but that it would not do for a medal". The Secretary observed that he felt quite sure that the Committee would very thankfully give every possible attention to any suggestion Mr. Pistrucci might favour them with. Mr. Pistrucci said "that he would not execute that design or any other design but his own" and asked who did the model. The Secretary explained "Mr. Clint Jnr". Mr. Pistrucci then lost his temper - very exceedingly angry, and exclaimed in a rage "that he would not do any design but his own". The Secretary then observed to Mr. Pistrucci, that when he had last the pleasure of conversing with him on the subject, he expressed himself willing to execute any design the Committee might furnish him with, whereupon Mr. Pistrucci replied - "tis false - I never said any such thing".

"The Secretary calmly observed, that he was sorry to see Mr. Pistrucci lose his temper - that his language was such as he, the Secretary, had never been accustomed to, that he called on him on the part of the Royal Humane Society, and that it certainly was his impression, that Mr. Pistrucci had expressed himself willing to execute any design furnished him by the Committee. Mr. Pistrucci again furiously reiterated "tis false - I will not execute any design that is not my own. I don't care for you, or the Treasurer, or the Chairman or the Committee or the President of the Humane Society, all together. They may do as they please, but they should either employ him or - emphatically slapping his trouser pocket - he would make them pay him for the medals. That he was not afraid of the Humane

Society or any other Society - or him, the Secretary - or any person in the world.

"The Secretary then observed in the same calm tone of voice, and the same quietness of demeanour - "not even Mr. Wyon" - Mr. Pistrucci's rage was then ungovernable, he approached the Secretary in a menacing manner, pulled open the door, and ordered him to quit the room. The Secretary refused to do so, observing, that he was sorry to see Mr. Pistrucci lose his temper and forget himself in the manner he had done. Mr. Pistrucci, disregarding the mild expostulation of the Secretary, persevered in a loud, angry, threatening tone of voice, in ordering the Secretary to go out of the room.

"The Secretary refused to leave the room unless Mr. Pistrucci requested him to do so in a gentlemanlike manner. Mr. Pistrucci then came up to the Secretary in a menacing attitude. The Secretary dared Mr. Pistrucci to lay a hand on him. Mr. Pistrucci, finding the Secretary determined not to leave, yet very quiet in his demeanour, sent for the warden: and upon his arrival, Mr. Pistrucci ordered him to turn the Secretary out of the Mint and on receiving the warden's order, the Secretary quietly left the room and the door was slammed to".

The end result of Westropp's account was that it finished Pistrucci's association with the Royal Humane Society, and shortly after its presentation Pistrucci asked to be paid £105 for his work, but he refused to allow the Society to have the models of the medal. Surprisingly on 19 August that year the Committee agreed to pay him in full. Perhaps some of them, or indeed a majority, did not agree with the action of their Secretary who undoubtedly brought about this sorry end?

My last comments on the Fothergillian Medal and of Pistrucci's association with it are quite simple, first I feel that the totally uncalled-for confrontation with Westropp was to say the least disrespectful, and the provocation was undoubtedly premeditated. However, I believe that Pistrucci was greatly provoked, and under the circumstances I feel he handled the situation quite well.

The work Pistrucci carried out on the replacement medal (Plate 21) met with considerable acclaim. On the obverse he altered the stance of the boy and achieved a better and more purposeful posture, while the reverse shows a much better spacing and the wreath is much more prominent. Another point well worth mentioning is that he also signed the medal in full on the obverse, and this was something he had done on several past occasions and been heavily criticised for it. Pistrucci was indeed a man who was very proud of his own work.

In 1830 Pistrucci engraved the medal of Sir Gilbert Blane (Plate 22), baronet and eminent physician. Blane himself established this prize medal in 1830 for the Royal College of Surgeons. Next in 1830 the first ever non-campaign medal was sanctioned for the British Forces, and the instructions to prepare it were given to Pistrucci in September of that year. He completed the medal in the following year, and received a fee of 100 guineas. Later in 1837 he updated the medal for Queen Victoria's reign (Plate 23) and was paid a further 100 guineas.

William IV succeeded his brother on the 26 June 1830 and prior to this Pistrucci as Chief Medallist had been asked to prepare the Coronation Medal, but it was to be copied from a Chantrey bust. As usual Pistrucci refused again to copy another artist's work; this time, the King refused to grant Pistrucci sittings, and the commission was passed to William Wyon. It seems that the year of 1830 saw Pistrucci pursue an interest in sculpture, and a very interesting article appeared in the [10]*Gentleman's Magazine* of that year. It relates to the Royal Academy Exhibition of 3 May 1830, and entry No 1167, a Capriccio by B. Pistrucci. It goes on to say "A block of marble has been chiselled by a most masterly hand into subjects without any connection with each other, we have Hercules, two or three busts on medallions, a female figure, above which there is a kind of grating through which are peeping fanciful and distorted heads. But, indeed, the affair defies minute description as much as it does criticism. The female figure is very lovely". I can only conclude by saying the writer more than likely saw as he wrote a superb block of marble.

10   Gentleman's Magazine June 1830. Vol. 100, p543. magnificent cameos.

In 1832 Pistrucci continued to devote some of his time to marble sculpture, and he cut a large portrait bust of the Duke of Wellington (Plate 24) for which he was given private sittings by the Duke. Over the next few years he carried out several more portrait busts of famous people, and of friends. In 1835 he produced a self-portrait bust (Plate 25) that displayed his name BENEDETTO PISTRUCCI across its base. Another notable bust of Pistrucci's was of Pozzo di Borgo, and this was really huge, being four times larger than life. The marble bust of Samuel Cartwright is perhaps one of his best works of sculpture, and in 1845 he cut a life-size portrait bust of his very close friend Archibald Billing. Some of Pistrucci's portrait busts are quite good, but his real forte in the cutting of stone was I feel achieved when he worked on those minute but magnificent cameos. Pistrucci continued with his work on cameos, and also on the Waterloo Medal. In February of 1836 Henry Labouchere first Baron Taunton, who was the Master of the Mint, said that he felt the Waterloo Medal should be finished, and Pistrucci was made an offer of £500 a year if he would take on four pupils and finish the medal. Pistrucci, still far from happy with his position, did not heed the offer.

This is a suitable moment to return to Pistrucci's work on cameos because at this time he cut two cameos of the Princess Victoria, the first of these an onyx of three strata, the outer two strata were white, and the middle stratum a dark brown. As a result of this sandwich effect he was able to cut on one side the young head bust of the Princess, and later when she became Queen he added on the other white side a new bust, this time with a diadem.

The second of the cameos (Plates 26 & 27) is one that I am most proud of because I had the great pleasure to discover it in 1985, and it has not until now been recorded. The cameo is oval in shape and cut on a sardonyx of two strata, one white and the other a rich dark brown; it measures 30 millimetres x 22 millimetres. It features, cut only in white, the very young bust of the Princess to the left, her hair bound with a double fillet and collected into a knot behind. The name PISTRUCCI is placed below the truncation on the dark brown field nearer the edge, and on a similar angle to that of the truncation. The actual detail is as one would expect from Pistrucci, and is certainly comparable to other superb cameos of his that I have seen. I have good reason to believe that this particular cameo can be traced back to the Duke of Wellington, who was in fact a very good patron of Pistrucci's.

An interesting cameo of Pistrucci's that I would like to mention in detail is n the Liverpool Museum Collection on Merseyside, mounted in gold on the id of a tortoiseshell snuff-box (Plate 28). The dimensions of the box are 25 millimetres high and 82 millimetres wide. The small oval cameo measures 38 millimetres x 29 millimetres and is cut on a sardonyx. It features the figure of Napoleon similar to the celebrated statue of him by Canova, and it s signed Pistrucci.

This snuff-box was once part of the well known Liverpool Collection of Joseph Mayer (1803-1886). Mayer subsequently sold it, together with the other Napoleonic miniatures, to John Mather of Liverpool, who, in 1872, gave the collection to the Liverpool Museum.

Mayer said that the cameo had been cut to the order of George IV, but unfortunately no evidence has been found of any such commission being placed by George IV either as Prince Regent or as King. Canova's statue was brought to England for presentation to the Duke of Wellington at a time when Pistrucci himself was in employment at the Royal Mint, and so it is very likely Pistrucci cut the cameo sometime after 1816 in England. The wax of the cameo has survived and is in the Museo Della Zecca of Rome. Mayer admired Pistrucci's work and wrote to him to enquire if he would accept a commission to cut either a portrait-medal or a marble bust. It seems that Mayer's enquiry did not progress, possibly because he felt Pistrucci's price was too high. Although Mayer's letter to Pistrucci has not survived his reply from Pistrucci has, and it is in the Fitzwilliam Museum collection at Cambridge. The letter, dated 8 February 1843, does not in my opinion indicate that Pistrucci's quoted figure of £105 was at all unreasonable. However, Mayer's collection included at least one superb Pistrucci item.

Another so far unrecorded cameo of Pistrucci's was discovered by Hancocks & Co Jewellers Ltd of London and they kindly passed on to me the details and photograph of it. The cameo (Plate 29) is oval and cut from agate of possibly three strata, and it is mounted in a superb oval shape gold brooch that measures 51 millimetres x 35 millimetres. The subject of the cameo is Amalthea holding a cornucopia of goat's milk and quenching the thirst of the infant Zeus, and it is signed PISTRUCCI just below the exergue line at the bottom. This is a beautiful and typical example of Pistrucci's work.

Here in Cambridge, we have another fine cameo of Pistrucci's housed in the Fitzwilliam Museum Collection. The cameo (Plate 30), cut from onyx of two strata, is signed by Pistrucci, and is an oval measuring 39 millimetres x 35 millimetres featuring the portrait of George IV as Prince Regent.

The cameo was given by the Friends of the Fitzwilliam in honour of Lady Butler of Saffron Walden, and purchased by the Fitzwilliam Museum with the aid of a contribution of £2,250 from the N.A.C.F. the regional fund administered by the Victoria and Albert Museum, and from Mr. Malcolm Carr of Hancocks. The cameo was purchased from Christies Sale, 26 June 1980 (Lot 153) at a cost of £9000.

There are two cameos in the Victoria and Albert Museum which I feel are of particular interest. The first is a delightful tiny piece known as Head of a Child (Plate 31). The child is the infant daughter of one of Pistrucci's best friends, Archibald Billing, and how beautifully Pistrucci has portrayed the chubby little child with her curly hair peeking out from under her bonnet. This cameo measures 19 millimetres x 16 millimetres, cut on sardonyx of two strata, the portrait being white and the base brown. The child later became Mrs. George Long and her daughter, Miss A.F. Long, bequeathed the cameo to the Victoria and Albert Museum in 1940.

The second cameo from the same collection is a shell cameo bearing the portrait bust of the Duke of Wellington, and attributed to Raphael Pistrucci (Plate 32). I have to say that this bust does convey to me some of the influence of the great Benedetto and is therefore very likely to be the work of his son Raphael, who was born in England and stayed here with his father for several years. The cameo measuring 58 millimetres x 43 millimetres was probably cut around 1850 and is an excellent likeness of the Duke of Wellington. It is almost certainly extremely rare.

Another lovely cameo of Pistrucci's is in the British Museum Collection, and it is the portrait bust of George III (Plate 33), cut from sardonyx of three strata and is signed Pistrucci, and was cut in 1816; it was later set in a plain gold pendant with gold rope edging. The cameo measures 31 millimetres high, and Pistrucci once more displays his expertise at using the different colours of the sardonyx to emphasise the hair and the toga. A similar version of this cameo was used by Thomas Wyon as a model for the 1816 gold guinea.

Chapter 8

As we move nearer to the reign of Queen Victoria I feel it is necessary to acquaint you more with the somewhat special relationship that Pistrucci enjoyed with Queen Victoria. He executed further work for the Queen in addition to the cameos I have just described, but when these were commissioned it was at that point his association with Victoria began, and he was in fact given several sittings by the then Princess for the cameos. She was delighted with Pistrucci's work, of which there is ample proof that he had achieved a real likeness in the portrait of the Princess. I was very privileged and fortunate in 1986 to meet Thomas Marquis Pistrucci, the great grandson of Benedetto. Tom spent nearly two weeks at my home as our guest and he talked to me a great deal of Pistrucci's association with Queen Victoria. I will write more later in this history about Tom.

Pistrucci was next commissioned in 1837 to cut the gold Coronation Medal for Queen Victoria (Plate 34); again he was given several private sittings by Victoria at Windsor and also at Brighton. Pistrucci again achieved an excellent likeness, and the Queen was pleased with his work, but as ever his enemies threw out the usual criticism which resulted in the Master being questioned about the medal in the House of Commons; the Master replied to the House that the suggested poor quality attributed to the medal was perhaps due to an illness that Pistrucci had suffered during his preparatory work on the medal. However, the medal was generally acknowledged to be a good design and he was paid a fee of £500.

In July 1838 the Mint was asked by the Court Jewellers Messrs Rundell, Bridge and Rundell for permission to produce a bronze medal of 86 millimetres. The obverse of this very large piece, weighing more than twenty five ounces was similar to that of the Coronation Medal, while the reverse bears the inscription DA/FACILEM CURSUM/ATQUE/ADNUE COEPTIS/1838 (Give an easy passage, and support our undertakings, 1838). Permission was also requested from the Master to have struck twenty four gold and twenty four silver shell medals of the obverse of this medal. The Mint granted permission for the medal and Pistrucci was instructed to proceed, and it has to be said that even though the medal was so large and heavy it was not a problem. Pistrucci was as proficient in hardening as well as engraving dies.

In 1838 Pistrucci was commissioned to make the seal of the Duchy of Lancaster, in silver and four inches in diameter. It features on the obverse the equestrian figure of the Queen, in high relief, and is surrounded by an inscription. The reverse displays the heraldic insignia of the Duchy. This magnificent seal was finished by Pistrucci in only fifteen days, and he said he was able to achieve this very rapid success by using a new process he had invented. If the seal had been executed by the old method whereby a wax model was made, and a copy taken from it by hand graving tools, then the seal would have taken several months of work before completion. Pistrucci's new method, which would enable great savings to be made, was very well detailed in a letter[11] that appeared in the *Numismatic Chronicle* of 1838-39 signed J.W.B and entitled "Pistrucci's Invention". I quote:

"Pistrucci's method is as follows:- He makes his design in wax or clay, imparting to his model the degree of finish he wishes finally to produce in metal: from this model a cast is made in plaster of Paris; which cast, having been hardened with drying oil, serves as a model from which an impression is very carefully taken in fine sand. From this a cast is made in iron; which iron cast Pistrucci employs as his die. It is obvious that by a very slight modification of his process, either a die or a punch is obtained: as it may be his object to produce a medal, or a seal, as in the case of the Duchy of Lancaster.

"The efficiency of this apparently unpromising contrivance depends on the following conditions and peculiarities:-
The cast iron die, prepared as above, is made extremely thin, - not exceeding, perhaps, one eighth of an inch; by which means, not only a degree of sharpness is obtained, similar, though certainly inferior to that produced by the Berlin workmen (and when I state that Pistrucci is his own founder, this will not appear extraordinary); but a degree of toughness and hardness, equal, if not superior to that of hardened steel, is acquired for the die, by its cooling in a mass, instead of cooling first on the two opposite surfaces, as is always the case with a large volume of metal, owing to the chill which necessarily affects the surface before extending to the interior; and of which

---

11   Numismatic Chronicle, Vol 1, 1838-39, pp53-62. Pistrucci's Invention by J.W.B.

the inevitable consequence is, that all the fine lines shrink, and the delicacy of the work becomes impaired, to say nothing of the fragility of the die itself produced under such conditions, which is an unsurmountable bar to its utility. The back of this thin cast-iron die is rendered mathematically smooth and even, and the edge made perfectly circular: and a corresponding circular hollow having been turned in a solid steel bed, into which the thin piece of cast-iron is inserted, all the advantages of weight and solidity are immediately imparted to it; at the same time that, owing to its thinness, it possesses, as already stated, the sharpness which could never have been imparted to an impression made in a thick or larger mass of metal.

"It requires very little discrimination to perceive that by this invention a gigantic stride has been made. No reflective mind can fail to have lamented, that the expense attending all original works of art must ever limit their production; and, among the rest, to have been frequently struck with regret at the melancholy conviction that the expense consequent upon the great labour and consumption of time in executing a medal, offers an insurmountable bar to our progress in this beautiful department of the fine arts. But Pistrucci shows us how the impediment is to be surmounted. By his invention - process - contrivance, or by whatsoever other name, or names, his friends or his enemies may please to designate his cheap method of procuring a first-rate die - we shall be able to multiply medals bearing original designs at a comparatively trifling expense."

I feel very much that this letter endorses even more the skills that we already know Pistrucci possessed, but as always the same old enemies of Pistrucci reared their ugly heads and wrote or voiced their ill-founded opinions of this great engraver. Once again though his work and achievements would answer his critics in no uncertain way, and as time went by others would reap the benefit from this Italian genius and his "new invention".

Another important event that occurred towards the end of this busy year of 1838 was the arrival of Pistrucci's ninth and final child, Benvenuto Benedetto, who was born on 14 October in London.

In October 1839 the Papal Government of Rome offered Pistrucci the post of Chief Engraver, and he left for Rome to take up the position. He remained in Rome for only a few months because he found the salary far too low, returning to England in 1840. Following this short stay in Rome he decided also to bring back to England his two younger daughters, Maria Elisa and Elena. Both the girls were keen on gem-engraving, and back at the Mint, under father's expert tuition, they soon became very successful. It was no surprise that quickly they began to command good fees for their work.

I think it is interesting to note at this point the [12]Royal Mint Census return of 1841, Whitechapel Registration District (June 6 quarter). It lists the following members of the Pistrucci family who were then in residence:

	Age	Occupation	Country
Benedetto Pistrucci	58	Sculptor	Foreigner
Barbara Pistrucci	56	Sculptor	Foreigner
Helena Pistrucci	18	Sculptor	English
Eliza Pistrucci	15	Sculptor	Foreigner
Bridgett Coulter	35	Servant	Ireland
Cathne Boil	25	Servant	Ireland

So the above Census report enables us to confirm that the Pistruccis had returned to England, and just in time to be included in the 1841 Royal Mint Census.

12   Census return for the Royal Mint, 6 June 1841.

Chapter 9

Pistrucci acquired two more commissions for medals in 1841, the first of these being the Duke of York Memorial Medal. Next to come was the Duke of Wellington Laudatory Medal (Plate 35) and this is one of my favourite Pistrucci medals. Its obverse features a magnificent bust of Wellington and the reverse displays the equally impressive device of the Corinthian Helmet with Bellerophon mounted upon Pegasus spearing the Chimaera.

By this time Pistrucci was doing very little other work at the Mint but at last his efforts and achievements were being recognised. He had gained important diplomas from the Royal Academy of Arts at Copenhagen, the Institute of France and the Academy of St. Luke in Rome. Over a very long period he had achieved a great deal of success for the Mint, and in 1842 he became an elected member of the Athenaeum Club. This was indeed a high testimonial of his character as an artist and also as a gentleman of great intellect. Billing himself described the honour as the equivalent to being elected F.R.S.

In 1843 Pistrucci continued in his same mode of work at the Mint, and again received praise for his work from various people, but no doubt that which he gained from the Mint would have pleased him most. It is appropriate to quote the relevant Mint correspondence[13] of 1843 from the British Library.

Jan 20
Signor Pistrucci

      The Master of the Mint presents his compliments to Signor Pistrucci, and takes the opportunity of informing him that her Majesty's Government have sanctioned the purchase from Messrs Rundell and Bridge of the die of the Queen's Head which was sold to three gentlemen by Signor Pistrucci and had recently been tendered by them to the Royal Mint. The Master of the Mint cannot refrain from expressing his high gratification at a circumstance which has made the Government become the proprietor of a beautiful and noble work.

---

13   British Library, Letters of Pistrucci, pp224 and 225, 1843.

Jan 23

Signor Pistrucci

The Master of the Mint presents his compliments to Signor Pistrucci and has the pleasure to acquaint him that an impression of the head of the Queen which the Mint has agreed to purchase from Messrs Rundell and Bridge, the work of Signor Pistrucci has been laid before H.R.H the Prince Albert, and that the Prince has been pleased to express his opinion that it is a work of great beauty, and the finest of that size which has been brought under his notice.

I think the die referred to in this Mint correspondence may well have been the very large one done by Pistrucci for Rundell & Bridge in 1838.

1844 was to prove an eventful year for Pistrucci, especially when the Audit Office began to query the expense of keeping him on at the Mint. William E Gladstone M.P. who was then Master decided to restore his salary to £350, and he also pressed Pistrucci further for the completion of the Waterloo Medal. In fact he offered Pistrucci £400 to finish the medal, but although more work was done it remained unfinished. Later in the year Pistrucci along with his two daughters, Maria Elisa and Elena, left their official Mint residence, and moved out of London. They took a cottage in Old Windsor known as "Fine Arts Cottage".

Pistrucci and his daughters spent almost six years in Old Windsor where they were able to enjoy a quiet and peaceful life together. Pistrucci welcomed the visits of his many friends from London, and these of course included his great friend William Hamilton.

He soon had his workroom organised and then began in earnest to finish the Waterloo Medal, and although he worked incessantly on the medal for long periods he was inactive for much of 1846. During this year he had a really bad fall on the cottage stairs. Finally in the year of 1849 he finished the Waterloo Medal and the balance of £1500 still remaining was paid to him. So at last the finest ever piece of intaglio work by any engraver was ready to be handed over to the Mint. It is I feel well worth quoting a letter of Pistrucci's along with notes and observations that appeared in the *Numismatic Chronicle* of 1849[14].

14   Numismatic Chronicle, Vol 12, 1849-50, pp115-122. Letter and Notes etc by Pistrucci

MR PISTRUCCI ON THE WATERLOO MEDAL - The following is the evidence of Mr. Pistrucci on the long looked for "Waterloo Medal", and the mechanical operations required in the striking of Medals generally. "I propose to call in person on Mr. Sheil, Master of the Mint, for the purpose of presenting to him my respects on the 1st day of January next year, 1849, and at the same time to place in his hands the two matrices of the great Waterloo Medal, given me to execute by the late Lord Maryborough when Master of the Mint, and on which I have employed the same diligence and perseverance which I have given to the most finished works which have issued from my hands. Inasmuch as I feel the greatest possible interest in the complete success of this work, unique, I may say, of its kind, for its dimensions and amount of labour, and on which I have spent a large portion of my life; and being most anxious that it should meet the public eye without delay, and without accident, I have taken the liberty to describe the method which I think ought to be followed in hardening the matrices, in polishing the table, and in striking the medal: this I have done without the most distant intention of offending anyone, or of dictating in what is the especial concern of those who will have to direct these mechanical operations. I therefore beg leave to transmit the accompanying paper in reply to the second part of the first question. This was prepared by me on the 15th of last month"

Notes and Observations of Benedetto Pistrucci on the best mode of hardening the Matrices of the Waterloo Medal, and also on other Mechanical operations which will be required for the successful striking of the Medals.

No 1. In the first place each matrix must be turned, to make the neck for holding the collar (the shorter the neck the better); the edge also must be turned, to form the border of the medal; this must be done by a very skillful and experienced turner, one on whom the most perfect dependence may be placed, that he will do it *bona fide*; for an accident produced by carelessness or inattention might in one moment entirely destroy the whole work, and without remedy: in truth, I can hardly say which of the two gives me most uneasiness, this simple operation of turning the matrices, or that of hardening them; for in the latter case a remedy might possibly be found for an accident, so as to save a good deal of work, perhaps all, by making punches.

No 2. It will be necessary to make two preparatory matrices in order to bring up the metal on the blanks, where it would be required; and thereby save the original matrices as much as possible: these should only be used when the metal shall have been previously well distributed by the *preparatory* matrices, which matrices ought to be constructed exactly in the same manner as those in which I have engraved the work. I make this suggestion simply because I think they would harden better than if each was of one piece, and each piece should be hardened separately; we shall then be able to see the changes, if any, which may be occasioned by the hardening. Here my own experience fails me, and I can only imagine what may be the effect; unfortunately I have never had it in my power to make experiments of the kind, owing to circumstances not necessary here to explain. I would wish, too, that an experiment should be previously made with two other matrices similarly constructed, which might be hardened without being separated; and we should then see if the centres came out perfectly hard, of which I have some doubt; nevertheless, after experiments of this nature, a safe judgement may be formed as to the best mode of proceeding to harden the originals, on which so much long and laborious work has been employed.

Some one, perhaps, will say: But why did you have these matrices made in two pieces, and not of one piece, as all matrices have been made heretofore, for the striking of medals? My answer will be, that the world has never yet seen a medal struck with so much work upon it, nor of such great dimensions, viz., of more than five inches in diameter. The one in question has on it no less than sixty figures, large and small; and I am quite certain, in case it should meet with an accident, that no one could take a punch from it, if each matrix was of one piece; though this might be done, now that is in two, with as much ease at least as would be compatible with the complicated work; I would further observe that my own experience has taught me that the centre of a matrix is always the most difficult part to harden, even where the diameter is but of ordinary dimensions; I should therefore say that it is in the highest degree difficult, if not almost impossible, to make the due degree of hardening enter into the centre of a matrix, almost seven inches in diameter; and it is clear that if the centre is not duly hardened, when it comes to receive the blows of the press, it will give way, and the effect of the work would be entirely spoiled.

As I write these memoranda simply for my own satisfaction, and not pretending to instruct those whose business it is to conduct operations of this nature, it neither being my duty to do it, nor being obliged to do it by my contract; I shall, however, proceed to put down on paper, without making any secret or mystery of it, the mode and means which I should adopt myself, in order to harden these two matrices with as much diligence and security as I could hope for. After I had made the experiments as above described, supposing that the separate hardening of the two pieces of each matrix proves to be successful, I would have an iron instrument made of this shape, which I would place in the centre of the ring, or outside piece, of the matrix before putting it in the iron pot, where it is to be imbedded in the animal charcoal, commonly called "hardening". This precaution I should take in consequence of the great weight and size of the matrix, nearly seven inches in diameter; which would render it otherwise extremely difficult and dangerous to take it out of the pot with sufficient rapidity, for it not to cool in its transit to the water; and also because the first impression or effect it would receive from the water would be by this contrivance much more *equal* than if the operator was to make use of the ordinary tongs, and there would be no danger of its slipping from the tongs. And in order to take it out of the pot with the same efficiency and security (without moving the pot itself, but merely taking the top off), I should pass an iron hook (with a long handle, about three feet long) through the hole of the instrument above described, and put the whole apparatus quite parallel into the water. The centre piece, which is of no great weight, might be taken out and hardened in the usual way. The mode I have always followed in hardening matrixes, whether for coins or for medals, has been to cover over the engraved surface, with a paste composed of wood, charcoal, and garlic, well pounded together in a mortar. In this way I have always preserved the matrixes from accidents which might occur, whether from the contact of the animal charcoal, or from that of the air, in their transit from the fire to the water; and the success has always been so complete, that the work has come out exactly as it was engraved, without the matrix being at all corroded by the fire, or oxygenated by the air. I do not pretend to teach anyone what does not belong to my own art, or what is purely mechanical, but my experience of so many years - all, I confess, acquired since I have been in England - encourages me to believe that my opinion may be of some value in a business of this nature. I cannot on any account undertake to conduct these

51

operations myself; it is much against my good will that I make this avowal; for I would willingly carry it on to the end with my own hands. But this great Waterloo medal has already passed, for no fault of mine, through so many disadventures, and it has caused me for a long series of years so many anxious thoughts, and so much intense study (connected too as it has been with the circumstances of the employments I have held in the Mint, and others), that I have no longer that confidence in myself, and in my own powers, which I should have had in operations of this nature, if I had continued to perform the duties of engraver in chief, and which I did possess, when I thought that, according to the promises held out to me, I should finish the medal in that employment. At that time it was my constant practice to harden with my own hands all the originals of coins as well as medals which were ordered of me by the Government, although I was bound by the duties of my office only to engrave them. I might adduce also many other reasons, and very strong ones too, arising from the change in my position in the Mint, which necessarily prevent me from reposing in others that full and entire confidence which ought to be given to those who would have to assist me in these various operations, some of which one man cannot do without help. The distribution of the presses, the rooms in which they are kept, the constant going to and fro of the workmen in these rooms; many of these being, as I have reason to believe, not well disposed towards me, nor likely to show much zeal in enabling me to produce a work which I flatter myself will secure to me the approbation of the Government; all these, and many other considerations, would make me apprehensive, and deprive me of that self-confidence which I have always hitherto had in every one of my former works. I therefore think it will be better for the public service that I should wash my hands of it, and leave what remains to be done in the hands of those to whom it belongs; and I feel assured that if they will use all necessary precautions, and give up for a time their whole mind and energies to this service, it will succeed in a manner to reflect honour upon the Mint, and will show what can be done by such a body of men when they are united. I am especially induced to feel confident of the result, from the fact that the two matrices are, I know, made of the very best steel; I have examined them over and over again, as much as human eye can do. In cutting into them, I have not discovered the smallest possible defect; and the observation was made when the hollow was cut out, to admit the centre piece, two three-quarter inches in diameter.

No 3. I would wish to say something on *the polishing of the field*, or *table* of the medal. This operation requires a workman of the greatest experience, and skill in polishing engraved matrices, one too in whom the most implicit confidence can be placed; for he may have it in his power to spoil all, by the very act of polishing the outlines, as well as the interior of the work; and I should wish to watch over him during this very important and delicate operation, in order to direct his proceedings, and to stop him if he is attempting to polish in a greater degree than is necessary at the first stage of the operation: the real polishing should only be given when the medals are in that state in which a single blow of the press is sufficient to complete them.

No 4. I cannot omit to take this opportunity to say a word on the subject of the presses now in the Mint, of the rooms in which they are placed, as also of the manner and degree of care which will be required when the medals are to be loosened from the matrices and collar, in order to prevent the possibility of any injury being done to the matrices while the medals are being struck, it being at all times well understood that the workman in charge of this operation is very well acquainted with and expert in his business. The workman in the Mint, Thomas Jerome, in whom I had implicit confidence, and who used to assist me, died two years ago.

The presses in the Mint applicable to strike medals are, I believe, three in number; but they have never been made use of to strike medals of the diameter above named; and, as when I received the commission to execute this medal, this difficult service was not provided for, but only talked of, as to be required at the time, now that the medal is finished, it will be necessary to think seriously about it. I believe that the diameter of the great screw now in use will be sufficient; also that the impetus given by the fly and weights attached to it will be enough for the medal in question; but I cannot vouch for it. It must also be observed that each of the matrices being in two pieces, viz., the centre and the ring, as is shown in the annexed section, it will be absolutely necessary that the field or lower plain of the press should be mathematically true, and exactly parallel with the upper plain of the same, which will have to bear the great force of the screw in giving the blow: if not, the blow will force the centre out of its place; and if this should occur, the matrices, one or both, will be instantly spoiled: this centre piece in each of the matrixes is in the slightest degree conical. An arrangement will also be necessary to spread the blow given by the nose of the screw equally over the whole surface of the medal. What press, then, it will be necessary to have for the striking of this large medal is a question which, in my capacity of Her Majesty's Chief Medallist, I do not, in truth, feel myself qualified to answer. I should have had more experience of this kind had I been continued in my first employment of chief engraver.

One of these presses is fixed in a room where the matrixes and punches of the coins are usually multiplied, and adjoining to another in which they are hardened. It is also one of the dirtiest places in the Mint; this is owing to the furnaces which are lighted in it; the great quantity of dust from charcoal, coke, and common coals; also from the number of persons continually passing to and fro, from the studio or apartments of the chief engraver above the room, and also from those of the clerk of the irons, whose room is similarly situated. I would also observe, that from the moment that the press selected for this service shall be adjusted to the state of perfection which is required, such adjustment must not be, in the slightest possible degree, altered, until the medals shall have been all struck. Any other arrangement would probably lead to very great inconveniences and injuries; for if the Master of the Mint were to allow such press to be used from time to time for other public services, and thus the striking of the medal be subjected to occasional interruptions, plausible pretexts would not be wanting to act on such permission, and much mischief would ensue, and everything would be put out of order, as, indeed, has frequently happened to me on other occasions. To exemplify this, it may be necessary to remind the reader that every medal will require a great many blows, and will frequently be taken from the press to be annealed, and on every such occasion the whole must be found exactly in *statu quo*; which could only be done after repeated trials if any alteration had been allowed in the arrangement of the press. These trials might injure the medals as well as the outlines of the engravings; and the more so as this press is now used night and day for the private medals manufactured by the chief engraver himself. It therefore seems to me useless to think of this press, which must also be the worse for wear for the many years it has been used to the chief engraver's profit.

The second press is one which Mr. Pole, when Master of the Mint, ordered to be made expressly for my use, and for multiplying the matrices and punches of the coins engraved by me, when I held the office of chief engraver. This was to enable me to make use of machinery in a state of perfection, and not injured by constant use in striking dies for the coins; and his intention was to place it in a room under my studio, all the officers of the Mint rose in opposition to the Master's orders, and he had the good nature to comply with their wishes; whereupon they replaced it in the turner's shop, where the matrices and all the dies are turned for striking the coins. Now, in the first place, this was a very dangerous spot for it, as there are always five or six workmen in the shop; secondly, it is at times the repository of all the punches and dies to be used for the coins; and, thirdly, it is liable to be entered by other persons; and, finally, it is a dirty place, ill kept; five or six workmen eat their meals in it, the operations of turning the dies are carried on there, and the floor is strewed with the shavings; any one of these, not bigger than a pin's head, might spoil a matrix while the medals were being struck. It would, therefore, I think, be difficult to use this press for the purpose in question; it would, at least, require to be most minutely examined, and none should be admitted into the shop but those actually engaged in striking the medal, which would be almost impossible.

There is also in the Mint a third press, that which is called the Prussian press, which Mr. Wallace ordered from Berlin, by the advice of Messrs Barton, Wyon &c.; but which after it had reached the Mint and had been paid for at a cost of four or five times as much as an English press would have cost, has never, to my knowledge, been used at all, the workmen not liking it, or not being able to use it. It remained in this state for many years, but those who advised this useless expense becoming apprehensive that when Mr. Labouchere became Master of the Mint the Government would inquire into the circumstance, the officers of the Mint determined to place it in a room belonging to the moneyers, to give it an appearance of being in use; but it was never used. At the time of the coronation of Her present Majesty I applied to Mr. Labouchere for permission to make use of it for the coronation medals. It was granted to me, and I used it with success, but I do not believe it has ever been used since that time, although during, I think, the administration of Mr. Labouchere's successor, the moneyers prevailed on the then Master of the Mint to order me to give up the key of the room in which it was kept and they resumed the custody of it, to let it be covered with rust, and that it should remain idle. I do not, however, believe that it would be possible to apply this Prussian press to the service in question, owing to circumstances which I could explain on the spot.

The above is the result of many anxious reflections on the subject during the last four years, which I have devoted uninterruptedly to the completion of the medal.

Finally, I wish to impress on all to whom this may come, that the individual who is to be charged with the duty of striking the medals, besides being eminently expert and skillful in his business, must give his serious thoughts to the manner in which the medals, after the several blows to which they have been subjected, may most easily and safely be liberated from the matrices and from the collar. These matrices weigh about 20 pounds each, and they must be raised perpendicularly every time that a medal is put under the press. If the utmost care is not taken in conducting this part of the operation, it may happen that the outlines of the figures may be scratched or abraded, and minute fragments of the matrix will stick to the medal. This may occur either from carelessness of the workmen, or from the adoption of an imperfect mode of releasing the medal from the matrix. There is no undercutting whatever throughout my work, and of this I can give proofs, if required, before I part with it. Again and again I recommend the importance, in separating the matrix from the medal, of not forcing it more on one side than on the other; the force must be perfectly equal and perpendicular.

I think I have now expressed all that occurs to me of importance on this subject; and I hope that God will grant me the consolation of seeing my great and laborious work happily struck and represented on a medal; likewise that Her Most Gracious Majesty, the Government, and the public in general, will see it precisely as I have engraved it.

P.S. I forgot to say that I should very much prefer that the medals should be struck, if possible, without preparatory dies; and that the dies which I have recommended above should only be made use of for experiments in hardening. I have offered the suggestion mainly from a feeling of anxiety to secure the very best mode of proceeding, if it should be found necessary.

What duties do you consider will remain for you to perform in the Royal Mint after the final completion of the Waterloo medal? - When I shall have placed, as above, the two matrices of the medal in the hands of the Master of the Mint, I consider that I return to the position in the Mint in which I was placed by the arrangement proposed and signed by the Right Honourable William Tierney, Master of the Mint in the year 1828, which constituted me his then Majesty's chief medallist in the Royal Mint, with a salary of 350l. a year, and by which, as far as I recollect the terms and spirit of it, I was to hold myself in readiness to execute any medals which should be ordered of me by any departments of the British Government, and for which I was to be compensated according to the scale of what had been previously paid to me for other works. I was also to bring up a pupil in my art, which I continued to do until I was deprived of a portion of my salary; but which I am ready to do now, if it should be required of me.

Chapter 10

In 1850, Pistrucci with his two daughters moved from Old Windsor and settled in a charming old Georgian home in Englefield Green, only a few more miles out of Windsor in a nice typically English village. The home was set in lovely rambling gardens that contained trees and shrubs in abundance, all of which must have given Pistrucci the quietness and tranquil kind of life that by now I am sure he very much desired. The name of the lovely old house was "Flora Lodge" (Plates 36 & 37). How significant the name was! I wonder if the great man himself chose the name of "Flora", that had such a bearing on his life.

I visited Flora Lodge in 1986 and took with me Tom Pistrucci to whom I referred earlier in this history. Tom had made the long trip from Australia where the family had settled in 1857. He had come to England to see for himself exactly where his famous great grandfather had spent so many years of his life. It was fortunate that we made the visit to "Flora Lodge" at that time because the lovely old house was demolished a year or so later.

Thomas Marquis Pistrucci has since passed away, and his sad death has in fact brought an end to the male side of the Pistrucci family. I can only say that it was so nice and a real pleasure to have Tom as a guest in my house in 1986, and how much we enjoyed several trips down "memory lane" during his stay. I feel at this point it is most appropriate to describe how the Pistrucci family got to Australia, and it was with much sadness and regret that I was unable to complete my work before Tom died. Tom contributed a great deal to the Australian part of my work, and enabled me to clarify several very grey areas.

Earlier in this history I mentioned the last born of Benedetto's children, a boy named Benvenuto Benedetto (Plate 38), who was born in Dalston in the Parish of St. John, London in 1838[15]. He grew up in London and eventually became a farrier, a trade he continued throughout his working life. Horses in fact much liked and appreciated by most of the Pistrucci family especially Benedetto. While still in his teens Benvenuto

---

15   Certificate of Birth, Hackney General Register Office, Middlesex, 1996.

met Mary Gorman, a young Irish girl from Wexford, and they married in the[16] Catholic Chapel in the District of St. George East, Middlesex on 23 March 1856. Shortly after, their first child William was born.

[17]In 1857 the family had obviously decided to leave England, and on 5 June in the steamship *Undaunted* they sailed from Portsmouth to Melbourne, Australia. Along with baby William they arrived in Melbourne on 20 August 1857, and so the Pistruccis were about to establish themselves in Australia.

Benvenuto (who later changed his name to Benjamin) and the family enjoyed a long life in Australia, with a further two generations that ended with Tom. Benvenuto/Benjamin Pistrucci died at the age of 88 and was buried in Bendigo Cemetery on 27 December 1926.

To return to the 1850s Benedetto Pistrucci now approaching seventy still remained very active, and continued to accept commissions for cameos and other things of interest. In spite of his age his sight remained good, and he did not need to use spectacles for such delicate and minute work that he continued to undertake.

His two daughters Maria Elisa and Elena who both had earlier received awards for the art of gem engraving from the Art Union Society of London, were still with him, and both were also kept busy with commissions. Needless to say they must have been wonderful company for the old maestro, and they undoubtedly kept Benedetto more than involved with their own work.

The last of his medal commissions was for the death of the Honourable J.C. Talbot Q.C and this he engraved in 1853. The bronze medal is 37 millimetres and the obverse displays Taylor's bust to the left, and the inscription reads

---

16   Certificate of Marriage, Tower Hamlets Register Office, Middlesex, 1996.
17   T.M. Pistrucci Archive (Author's collection).

JOHANNES CHETWYND TALBOT SVI MEMORES ALIOS MERENDO FECIT (John Chetwynd Talbot made others mindful of him by his deserts) the reverse NOVA·VIRTUTE·PVER·MACTE (You are honoured, my son, for your youthful courage). In the centre: CIↃ.IↃCCC.L.III. The medal is extremely rare.

The Honourable John Chetwynd-Talbot Q.C (1806-52) was a very distinguished man. He was the fourth son of the second Earl Talbot, Attorney General to the Prince of Wales, and also the Recorder of Windsor. So an important medal for Pistrucci to end his medal career.

The year of 1854 must have been a sad one for Pistrucci to bear when he was given the news that his son Camillo had died of cholera in Rome. He was only forty three years of age. But for Benedetto himself the end was also near, and in 1855 the great engraver carried out his last work. The year saw the visit of Napoleon III to England and Pistrucci's final work was to model two waxes for the occasion (Plates 39 & 40); it is only fitting that they were as good as his modelling in wax always was, and they are preserved in the Museo Della Zecca collection in Rome. Benedetto Pistrucci, Chief Medallist to Her Majesty died on 16 September 1855 aged seventy two. His cause of death was certified as bronchitis. On 20 September he was laid to rest in the lovely church grounds (Plate 41 & 42) in the Parish of Christ Church, Virginia Water in the County of Surrey. (Plate 43) The Church Burial Register shows the entry of Benedetto's death No 174.

My final comments on Pistrucci's career involve the many problems presented by his London critics and rivals. I have already mentioned that his rivals were, in the main, members of the Wyon family, but I must make it clear that I cannot find any evidence to suggest that William Wyon would have been a party to this. Although both Wyon and Pistrucci had their differences I am sure that had they been left alone even better results would have been achieved. Wyon, although without the classical and inventive background of Pistrucci, went on to become a very successful medallist, and indeed the first medallist to be elected a member of the Royal Academy.

Over his long and often arduous career in which he was known many times to work up to fifteen or twenty hours a day, Pistrucci's achievements were in my view beyond question. I have already described in detail his work on coins, medals and cameos, and in those areas no more is necessary.

However, his greatest work of engraving must be that of the Waterloo Medal matrices, and no better piece of intaglio engraving or design has surely ever been seen before or since. It contains as much as thirty ordinary-sized medals, and this alone was more than most medallists achieved in a life time. My last mention in this summary of his work and achievements must be of the Gold Sovereign, and his superb classical design of St. George slaying the Dragon. It is indeed a tribute that his wonderful design should still adorn the gold coinage of our current Queen Elizabeth II. It is one of the finest ever in our coinage history, and has certainly stood the test of time. Long may it continue.

Pistrucci's success has indeed been recognised by others, and apart from those I have already mentioned he was given diplomas by the Academy of St. Luke of Rome, the Royal Academy of Art Copenhagen, the Academy of Art Bologna, the Academy of Art Brussels and the Institute of France.

To honour the memory of Pistrucci the municipality of Rome has given his name to a street in the city, quite close to the Palazzo di Giustizia and overlooking the river Tiber (Plate 44).

My closing comments on this great man are these. I have been fortunate enough to see, and in most cases examine, many of Pistrucci's works. Be it medals, coins, waxes, cameos or whatever, I have seldom been anything but elated with what I have seen, and my admiration for Benedetto Pistrucci has steadily risen. For me he had no equal of the nineteenth century, and before him perhaps only Benvenuto Cellini was comparable.

How lucky we were to have him in England for some forty years and how much he contributed to what we might all regard as a Golden Age of Numismatic Design.

PLATES

Plate 1

Napoleon I wax portrait bust by Pistrucci.

Plate 2

The Flora cameo from the Payne Knight collection
by Pistrucci. Length 23 millimetres.

Plate 3

George III jasper cameo for the Sovereign c1816
signed Pistrucci. Actual size 22 millimetres.

Plate 4

George III jasper cameo for the Shilling c1816
by Pistrucci. Actual size 24 millimetres.

Plate 5

George III jasper cameo for the Half-Crown c1816
signed Pistrucci. Actual size 38 millimetres.

Plate 6

Obverse and Reverse of George III gold Sovereign 1817
by Pistrucci. Actual size 22 millimetres.

Plate 7

Obverse and Reverse of George III gold Five Pounds 1820 (Proof)
by Pistrucci. Actual size 33.5 millimetres.

Plate 8

Obverse and Reverse of George III gold Two Pounds 1820 (Proof)
by Pistrucci. Actual size 27 millimetres.

Plate 9

Obverse and Reverse of George III silver Crown 1818
ANNO REGNI LVIII by Pistrucci. Actual size 38 millimetres.

Plate 10

Courtesy of
The Author's Collection.

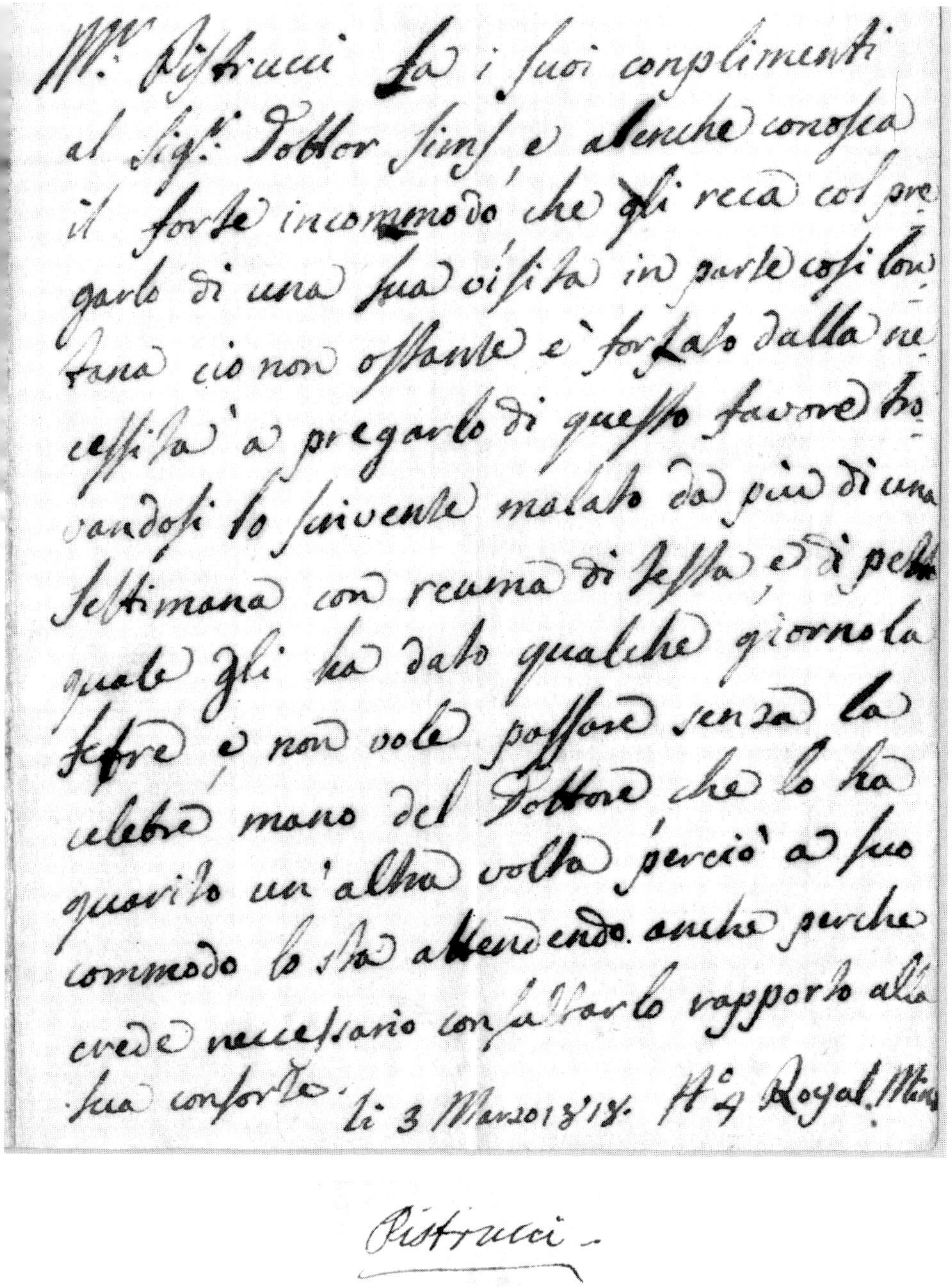

Mr. Pistrucci fa i suoi complimenti
al Sigr. Dottor Sims, e abenche conosca
il forte incommodo che gli reca col pre
garlo di una sua visita in parte così lon
tana ciò non ostante è forzato dalla ne
cessità a pregarlo di questo favore tro
vandosi lo scrivente malato da più di una
settimana con reuma di testa, e di petto
quale gli ha dato qualche giorno la
febre e non vole passare senza la
celebre mano del Dottore che lo ha
guarito un'altra volta perciò a suo
commodo lo sta attendendo. anche perche
crede neccessario consultarlo rapporto alla
sua conforto. li 3 Marzo 1818. No. 4 Royal Mint

Pistrucci -

An original letter written by Pistrucci on 3rd March 1818 to Dr Tobler.

Plate 11

49/50 by Pistrucci.

Plate 12

The Waterloo Medal wax model by Pistrucci. Obverse

Plate 13

The Waterloo Medal wax model by Pistrucci. Reverse

Plate 14

Obverse and Reverse of George IV gold Coronation Medal 1821
by Pistrucci. Actual size 35 millimetres.

Plate 15

Obverse and Reverse of George IV gold Sovereign 1825
by Pistrucci. Actual size 22 millimetres.

Plate 16

Obverse and Reverse of George IV silver Crown 1821
by Pistrucci. Actual size 38 millimetres.

Plate 17

Courtesy of
The Royal Mint.

Uniface Portrait medallic plaque of Benedetto Pistrucci 1826
by C. F. Voigt Gilded Bronze. Actual size 86 millimetres.

Plate 18

Uniface Portrait medallic plaque of Benedetto Pistrucci 1826
by C. F. Voigt Gilded Bronze. Actual size 86 millimetres.
This plaque is from the Grand Duke of Baden Cabinet, No. 4122,
and together with the Royal Mint plaque (Plate 17) they are
the only known examples of this superb Pistrucci bust by Voigt.

Plate 19

Obverse and Reverse of Death of Taylor Combe Medal 1826
by W. J. Taylor after B. Pistrucci. AE. Actual size 46 millimetres.

Plate 20

Obverse and Reverse of Death of Duke of York Medal 1827
by Pistrucci. AE. Actual size 60 millimetres. (Thomas Hamlet)

Plate 21

Royal Humane Society Medal 1839
by Pistrucci. AE. Actual size 51 millimetres.

Plate 22

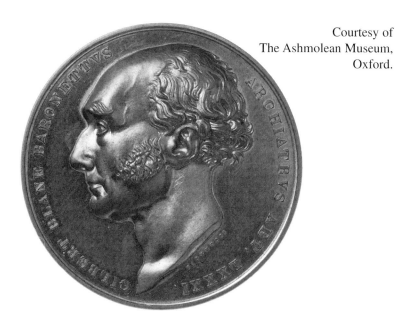

Obverse and Reverse of Sir Gilbert Blane Medal 1830
by Pistrucci. AV. Actual size 38 millimetres.

Plate 23

Obverse and Reverse of Victoria Long Service
and Good Conduct Medal 1838
by Pistrucci. AR and with maroon riband.
Actual size of medal 36 millimetres.

Plate 24

Duke of Wellington marble bust 1832 by Pistrucci.

Plate 25

Self-portrait bust of BENEDETTO PISTRUCCI.

Plate 26

The Princess Victoria cameo c1836 by Pistrucci on sardonyx.
Actual size 30 millimetres x 22 millimetres, signed Pistrucci.

Plate 27

The Princess Victoria cameo (No. 26), but shown
in contemporary gold and leather fitted case.

Plate 28

Courtesy of
The Liverpool Museum.

Napoleon I cameo mounted in gold and set in a tortoiseshell snuff box.
Actual size of cameo 39 millimetres x 29 millimetres, signed Pistrucci.

Plate 29

Courtesy of
Hancocks & Co. (Jewellers) Ltd,
London.

Amalthea and the infant Zeus cameo on agate and set in a gold brooch.
O/A size of brooch 51 millimetres x 35 millimetres, signed Pistrucci.

Plate 30

Courtesy of
The Fitzwilliam Museum,
Cambridge.

George, Prince Regent of England cameo c1817-1820 on onyx.
Actual size 40 millimetres x 35 millimetres, signed Pistrucci.

Plate 31

Head of a child cameo (Daughter of Billing) on sardonyx.
Actual size 19 millimetres x 16 millimetres, signed Pistrucci.

Plate 32

Duke of Wellington cameo c1850 on shell.
Actual size 58 millimetres x 43 millimetres.
Attributed to Raphael Pistrucci.

Plate 33

George III cameo 1816 on sardonyx and in later gold pendant.
Actual height of cameo 31 millimetres, signed Pistrucci.

Plate 34

Obverse and Reverse of Victoria gold Coronation Medal 1838
by Pistrucci. Actual size 36 millimetres.

Plate 35

Obverse and Reverse of Duke of Wellington Laudatory Medal 1841
by Pistrucci.AE. Actual size 61 millimetres.

Plate 36

The author at the entrance to 'Flora Lodge' 1986.

Plate 37

Tom Pistrucci at the entrance to 'Flora Lodge' 1986.

Plate 38

Benvenuto Pistrucci in Australia c1900.

Plate 39

The visit to England by Napoleon III.
Wax model by Pistrucci.

Plate 40

The visit to England by Napoleon III.
Wax model by Pistrucci.

Plate 41

Benedetto Pistucci's grave at Virginia Water.
Inscription on tombstone reads:

BENEDETTO PISTRUCCI
HER MAJESTY'S CHIEF MEDALLIST
STATUARY,
AND SCULPTOR OF GEMS
BORN IN ROME 24TH MAY 1783
DIED AT ENGLEFIELD GREEN
16TH SEPTEMBER 1855.

Plate 42

Benedetto Pistrucci's grave at Virginia Water.

Plate 43

Name.	Abode.	When buried.	Age.	By whom the Ceremony was performed.
George Chapman No. 169	Virginia Water	April 2	5	Thomas Brodie
Mary Drake No. 170	St Annes Heath	April 26	59	Thomas Brodie
Joseph Shanks No. 171	St Annes Heath	May 1st	43	Thomas Brodie
Anny Jennings No. 172	Virginia Water	June 18	16	Thomas Brodie
Sarah White No. 173	Stroud	Sept 4th	68	Edward Lett
Benedetto Pistrucci No. 174	Egham	Sept 20th	72	John B. Mowser Vicar
Thomas Tripp No. 175	Stroude	Sept 27th	30	John B. Mowser Vicar
Sophia Green No. 176	Wentworth Farm	November 1st	29	Thomas Brodie

The burial register of Virginia Water Church.

108

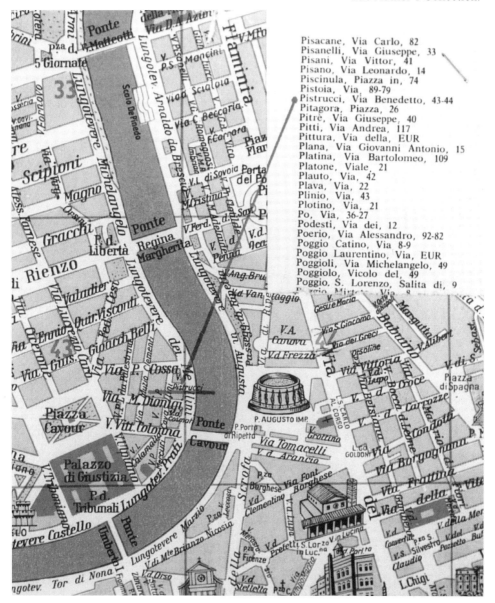

Plate 44

Courtesy of
The Author's Collection.

Pisacane, Via Carlo, 82
Pisanelli, Via Giuseppe, 33
Pisani, Via Vittor, 41
Pisano, Via Leonardo, 14
Piscinula, Piazza in, 74
Pistoia, Via, 89-79
Pistrucci, Via Benedetto, 43-44
Pitagora, Piazza, 26
Pitré, Via Giuseppe, 40
Pitti, Via Andrea, 117
Pittura, Via della, EUR
Plana, Via Giovanni Antonio, 15
Platina, Via Bartolomeo, 109
Platone, Viale, 21
Plauto, Via, 42
Plava, Via, 22
Plinio, Via, 43
Plotino, Via, 21
Po, Via, 36-27
Podesti, Via dei, 12
Poerio, Via Alessandro, 92-82
Poggio Catino, Via 8-9
Poggio Laurentino, Via, EUR
Poggioli, Via Michelangelo, 49
Poggiolo, Vicolo del, 49
Poggio, S. Lorenzo, Salita di, 9

A map of central Rome showing the street
(Via Pistrucci) named in Pistrucci's honour.

Plate 45

Obverse and Reverse of the William Wellesley Pole Medal 1823
by Pistrucci. Actual size 51 millimetres.

Plate 46

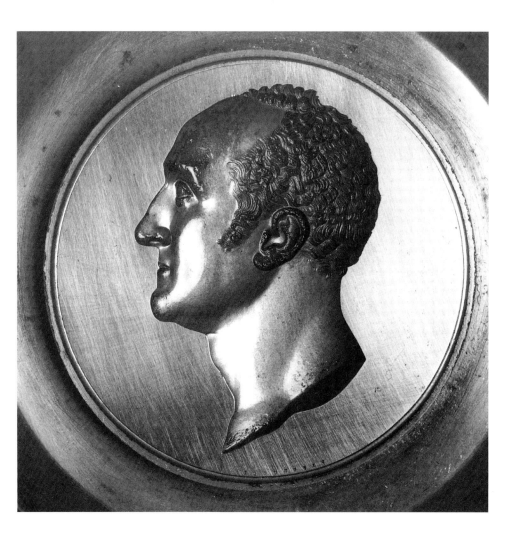

The obverse die for the William Wellesley Pole Medal of 1823
by Pistrucci. Actual size 48 millimetres.

Plate 47

William Wellesley Pole Medal 1823.
A lead trial striking of the obverse.

Plate 48

Roman Emperor Augustus cameo c1830 on agate and mounted in
enamel and chased gold setting.
O/A height 50 millimetres, signed Pistrucci.

Plate 49

The Waterloo Medal. Electrotype.
Actual size 136 millimetres. Obverse.

Plate 50

Courtesy of
The Royal Mint.

The Waterloo Medal. Electrotype. Reverse.

Plate 51

The Waterloo Medal. Brown wax impression. Obverse.
Taken at the Royal Mint 1980. Actual size 134 millimetres.

Plate 52

The Waterloo Medal. Brown wax impression. Reverse.

Plate 53

St. George slaying the Dragon. Wax model by Pistrucci for the Sovereign.
This model was purchased by Captain Bruce Ingram, O.B.E., at a sale in
Rome and later kindly given by him to the British Museum.
(B.M.Quarterly Vol 7 1932-33)

Plate 54

The Benedetto Pistrucci Medal 1993-94. Actual size 55 millimetres, in
AE, AR and Guilded Bronze. Obverse by Avril Vaughan. Reverse by John
Lobban. This medal was first issued under the auspices of the Society of
Numismatic Artists and Designers. The Society was formed in 1990 and
the medal was struck by Thomas Fattorini in Birmingham.

Plate 55

Courtesy of
The Royal Mint.

A proud moment for Thomas Pistrucci as he stands at one of the
doorways leading into the Royal Mint in London 1986.

Plate 56

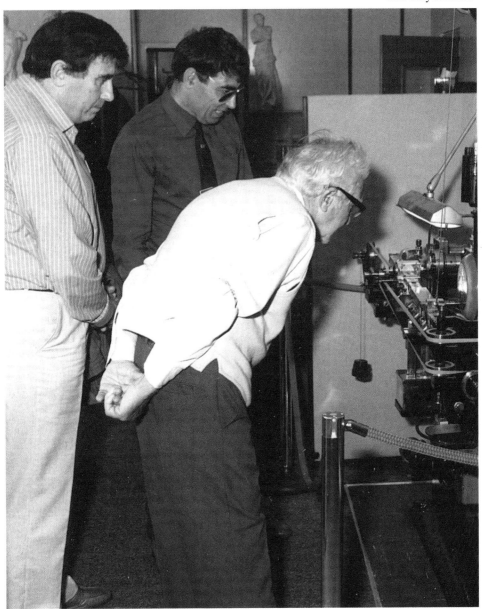

Derek Gorringe, the Deputy Chief Engraver (centre) explains
the reducing machine to the author (left) and Thomas Pistrucci
at the Royal Mint in 1986.

Plate 57

Thomas Pistrucci admiring the Waterloo Medal Matrices
at the Royal Mint in 1986.

SELECT BIBLIOGRAPHY

BILLING, Archibald, *The Science of Gems, Jewels, Coins and Medals*,
New Edition, 1875

BROWN, Lawrence, *A catalogue of British Historical Medals 1760-1960*
Vol 1, 1980

BROWN, Lawrence, *A catalogue of British Historical Medals 1837-1901*
1987

CHALLIS, C.E. (ed.), *A New History of the Royal Mint*   C.U.P. 1992

CRAIG, Sir John, *The Mint*. A History of the London Mint from
A.D. 287 to 1948   C.U.P. 1953

CULLIMORE ALLEN, J.J., *Sovereigns of the British Empire*   London 1965

DOUGLAS-MORRIS, Capt. K.J.,R.N., *Catalogue of English Gold Coins
1700-1900*   London 1974

DUVEEN, Sir Geoffrey & STRIDE, H.G., *The History of the Gold Sovereign*
London 1962

DYER, G.P., *Royal Sovereign 1489-1989 3 The Modern Sovereign*   1989

FORRER, L., *Biographical Dictionary of Medallists*   B. Pistrucci
London 1906
The Wyons
London 1917

GATTY, Charles T., *Catalogue of Mediaeval and Later Antiquities
contained in the Mayer Museum, Liverpool*   1883

GIBSON, Margaret & WRIGHT, Susan M., *Joseph Mayer of Liverpool
1803-1886*   1988

JONES, Mark, British Numismatic Journal, Vol.54. The Fothergillian Medal
1984

KING, C.W., *Antique Gems and Rings*   London 1872

MARSH, Michael A., *The Gold Sovereign*   Cambridge 1980

MARSH, Michael A., *The Gold Half Sovereign*   Cambridge 1982

MONTAGU, H., *Catalogue of Milled English coins, including Patterns and Proofs*   London 1891

MURDOCH, J.G., *Catalogue of Coins and Medals* Third Portion
London 1904

PISTRUCCI, Benedetto, Numismatic Chronicle, Vol.12
Notes and Observations   London 1849-50

POLLARD, J. Graham, *Benedetto Pistrucci in Inghilterra*   1981
Matthew Boulton and the Reducing Machine in England   1971

STEFANELLI, Lucia Pirzio Biroli, Bollettino di Numismatica Monografia,
Museo Della Zecca. Vols 1 & 2
I Modelli in Cera di Benedetto Pistrucci   Rome 1989

J. W. B., Numismatic Chronicle, Vol.1 *Pistrucci's Invention* London 1838-39

H. M. The Art Journal   November 1849

Allgemeine Deutsche Biographie   Leipzig 1896